Switzerland
French–speaking areas

By the staff of Editions Berlitz

How to use our guide

- All the practical information, hints and tips that you will need before and during the trip start on page 101.
- For general background, see the sections The Region and the People, p. 6, and A Brief History, p. 12.
- All the sights to see are listed between pages 18 and 83. Our own choice of sights most highly recommended is pinpointed by the Berlitz traveller symbol.
- Entertainment, nightlife and all other leisure activities are described between pages 83 and 92, while information on restaurants and cuisine is to be found on pages 92 to 100.
- Finally, there is an index at the back of the book, pp. 126–128.

Although we make every effort to ensure the accuracy of all the information in this book, changes occur incessantly. We cannot therefore take responsibility for facts, prices, addresses and circumstances in general that are constantly subject to alteration. Our guides are updated on a regular basis as we reprint, and we are always grateful to readers who let us know of any errors, changes or serious omissions they come across.

Text: Ken Bernstein
Photography: Claude Huber
Layout: Doris Haldemann
We're especially grateful to the Swiss National Tourist Office, Peter Kuhn, and the local tourist offices in Fribourg, Geneva, Lausanne, Neuchâtel and Sion, for their help in providing information for this book.
Cartography: © 1982, Hallwag Ltd., Berne, Switzerland

Contents

Cover picture: The village of Saint-Saphorin by the Lake of Geneva.

The Region and the People

Unlike those intriguing Swiss bank accounts, the nation's visible marvels are numberless: peaks covered with eternal snow, deep green valleys, medieval castles and tidy villages. And don't forget the famous cheese, chocolate and clocks. Everything is squeezed into less than 16,000 square miles; two Switzerlands would fit neatly into Ireland.

Deep cultural currents converge at this landlocked linguistic crossroads. Three major European languages are offici-

ally used in Switzerland. Sixty-five percent of the people speak a species of German; 18 percent claim French as their mother tongue; and 12 percent (including immigrants from south of the border) speak Italian. A fourth language, Romansh, is proudly preserved by about one percent of the population, mostly in isolated eastern districts. Switzerland has so many official names—Schweiz, Suisse, Svizzera—that the coins and postage stamps identify it in Latin: Helvetia.

Valais village girls in festive finery scamper over the cobblestones; cycling through Jura farm country.

This book covers the French-speaking region, the western fourth of the country, known as Suisse Romande*. Here the heart inevitably leans toward Paris but the Swissness scarcely relents: Lausanne's Métro trains depart every $7\frac{1}{2}$ minutes—by the second-hand!

French-speaking Switzerland has no single cultural or political capital. Its biggest city, Geneva, was the Rome of the Protestant world in the 16th century, but some other parts of Suisse Romande remain solidly Catholic. The linguistic and religious divergences among the Swiss usually balance out in peaceful coalitions and compromises.

Geneva's setting is superb—aristocratic houses and gardens astride the narrow tip of the biggest lake in the Alps. Over the years, the Lake of Geneva (the correct name is Lac Léman) has attracted a good deal of foreign talent: Byron, Gogol, Stravinsky, Nabokov, Charlie Chaplin. The lake also supplies inspiration to the likes of the Aga Khan and the Emir of Qatar... and ordinary tourists who don't require a palace to appreciate the reflections of the Alps in its deep, sparkling but changeable waters.

The principal port on this international lake (you can sail over to France for lunch!) is Lausanne, capital of the populous canton of Vaud and world headquarters of the Olympic games. Both Geneva and Lausanne have important cathedrals and universities. Other towns of the region have their own religious or intellectual traditions superimposed on enthralling scenery. Fribourg perches above a deep winding river. Neuchâtel sprawls along its own lake. Sion, in Valais, lives beneath a pair of surrealistic humped hills, themselves dwarfed by surrounding Alps.

Not everything is monumental or serious. At the eastern end of the Lake of Geneva, on the almost tropical shore known as the Vaud Riviera, flower-bedecked Montreux plays host to celebrated music festivals. Inland, in the tiny trim village of Gruyères, folklore and cheese make the world go round. And in almost any town you may stumble upon local seasonal festivals enlivened by authentic costumes, flowers and the blare of brass bands.

* The eastern and central regions of the country are covered in a companion Berlitz guide: SWITZERLAND: GERMAN-SPEAKING AREAS

8

Market day: the freshest flowers, crispest cabbages, sleekest leeks.

Fine ensemble of low-rise buildings grace the Right Bank of Geneva.

Unless you're addicted to museums and historic churches —with which the region is bountifully supplied—you'll probably spend most of your time outdoors in the deliciously pure air. The choice of activities, from lazy to strenuous and daring, couldn't be bigger. Climb a mountain or ride a horse. Ski (the year round!) or play tennis or golf. Swim or sail, water-ski or fish. Or stroll at your own pace through the verdant countryside.

Between energetic outbursts you can settle down in a park or café and watch the Swiss: athletic-looking women with overfed dogs, well-mannered children greeting you with a *"Bonjour, monsieur (or madame)"*, neatly uniformed street-cleaners operating mechanical scrubbers which shine the pavements, less neatly uniformed citizen-soldiers lugging their automatic rifles off to a spell of training. Yes, strangely enough, neutral, peaceful Switzerland bristles with permanent preparations against any foreign attack— tanktraps, camouflaged bunkers, airstrips hidden in bucolic valleys with underground park-

ing for the jets, and an army reserve of every able-bodied male up to the age of 50.

The man in the street not only defends his country but takes a big part in running it. Swiss direct democracy puts more power in the hands of the individual citizen, the town and the canton (state) and less at the centre. Local initiatives propose new laws and popular referendums approve or reject them.

Although the French-speaking Swiss tend to take life more casually than their compatriots in German-speaking Zurich or Basel, pedestrians still wait interminably for the traffic light to change, rather than jay-walk across an empty street. Residents of Montreux receive an official seven-page illustrated booklet explaining how, where and when to dispose of rubbish. All this order and organization seems even more remarkable when you consider that nearly one out of every six inhabitants is a foreigner: a political exile, a "guest worker" or a tax-sensitive film star.

The Swiss standard of living is enviably high: per-capita income far exceeds that in the United States. Moreover, this prosperity has been attained with almost no conventional natural resources. It's Swiss in-

11

genuity and perfectionism that makes the difference.

But industriousness, thrift and discretion don't interfere with good times. Even in Calvin's Geneva the nightclub patrons frolic far into the night. And by way of simple pleasures you can stop in any café and try the wine from just up the hill—unassuming as a mountaineer's hut. As for the food, local cooks rarely strive for gourmet productions, but they turn out home-style food you'll like. The quantity, though, is almost overwhelmingly generous. If Swiss cuisine consisted of nothing more elaborate than the cheese, it would still be a winner.

In all the bigger towns the shop windows are seductive: gold watches and jewellery, furs and fashions. If your budget keeps you outside looking in, you can still enjoy all the colour of a street market. Once or twice a week almost every town and village has an outdoor bazaar—freshly picked flowers, fruits and vegetables, home-made sausages and bread.

You may never want to leave this little, well-ordered world of scenic grandeur where hospitality, good food and drink are served up with admirable efficiency.

A Brief History

The story of Switzerland has a happy ending—liberty, peace and prosperity. But first came centuries of struggle against nature and hostile neighbours.

Cave-men inhabited Switzerland 10,000 years ago, picking berries, hunting reindeer and trying to elude the tusks of wandering mammoths. After another 5,000 years of development, neolithic settlers built stilt houses around Alpine lakes, grew grain and raised livestock.

During the second Iron Age, around 400 B.C., Celtic tribesmen arrived from the north with a more advanced culture. They were called Helvetians, and from them derives the original name of Switzerland, Helvetia.

Surrounded by hostile Germanic tribes, the Helvetians initiated a scorched-earth policy, burning their farms and houses and emigrating en masse across Gaul. But Roman legions, commanded by Julius Caesar, blocked their path in 58 B.C. The Helvetians, about whom Caesar wrote flattering reports, were forced to return home. Under Roman control the old Helvetian town of Aventia became Aventicum, administrative centre of Ro-

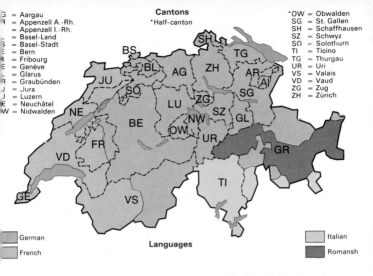

Cantons

*Half-canton

AG = Aargau
AR = Appenzell A.-Rh.
AI = Appenzell I.-Rh.
BL = Basel-Land
BS = Basel-Stadt
BE = Bern
FR = Fribourg
GE = Genève
GL = Glarus
GR = Graubünden
JU = Jura
LU = Luzern
NE = Neuchâtel
NW = Nidwalden

*OW = Obwalden
SG = St. Gallen
SH = Schaffhausen
SZ = Schwyz
SO = Solothurn
TI = Ticino
TG = Thurgau
UR = Uri
VD = Vaud
VS = Valais
ZG = Zug
ZH = Zürich

Languages

German

French

Italian

Romansh

man Switzerland. Imperial Aventicum, nearly 60 kilometres north-east of the Roman trading post of Lousonna (now Lausanne), is today's sleepy village of Avenches.

The Romans built international roads through Switzerland, bringing the latest technology and culture and, eventually, the new religion of Christianity. With the collapse of the Roman empire, the Burgundians moved into western Switzerland, while the east fell to the Alemanni, fierce Germanic tribesmen. This dividing line between the Burgundians and the Alemanni, along the Sarine River, still more or less

forms the linguistic frontier between French-speaking and German-speaking Switzerland.

The Middle Ages

Switzerland was briefly united under Charlemagne's Holy Roman Empire in the 9th century, but all Europe soon splintered into feuding feudal city-states, dukedoms and family fiefs. By the middle of the 13th century, two powers predominated: the House of Savoy and the Habsburgs. In central Switzerland local resistance to the widening Habsburg power led to a mutual assistance pact in 1291 between the communities of Uri, Schwyz and Unterwald, which **13** snowballed over the next century into a full-fledged confederation of eight cantons united against all foreign perils. This was the era of William Tell, who shot an apple from the head of his small son at 100 paces. Actually, discrepancies in the story of Tell, ace archer and foe of tyrannical overlords, prompt some critical historians to believe Switzerland's greatest hero was just a myth.

Nobody, though, doubts the courage and prowess of medieval Swiss soldiers. They impressed invaders so often that a new export trade began: Swiss troops hired out as mercenaries, sometimes on both sides of a war. The sight of these tough peasants with their heavy, deadly halberds was an important psychological weapon. Descendants of the halberdiers, in medieval finery,

Picture of defeat: with the Swiss in hot pursuit, Charles the Bold of Burgundy flees 1476 battlefront.

may still be seen on guard at the Vatican … the only Swiss warriors in foreign service today.

The best advertisement for Swiss military efficiency may have been Charles the Bold, the hard-hitting Duke of Burgundy. He lost two disastrous battles to the Swiss in 1476. At Grandson, on Lake Neuchâtel, Swiss troops routed the duke and his army; he is said to have decided to retreat when he heard the ghastly sound of a Swiss horn. Looking for re-

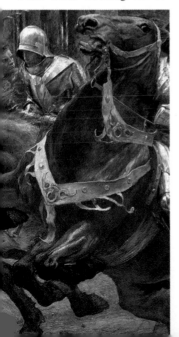

venge, the brave duke laid siege to the walled town of Morat, about 40 kilometres away as the arrow flies. A vast Swiss relief column came to the rescue of the Morat garrison, thrashing the Burgundians and pursuing them without mercy. It was a notable massacre. The duke's fortunes continued to decline and he was killed the following year in the battle of Nancy. The Swiss remember Grandson and Morat with unconcealed pride.

Overcoming Setbacks

The seemingly invincible Swiss split forces (half of them settled with François Iᵉʳ and returned home) and met defeat in 1515, at the hands of the French, in the battle of Marignano (Italy). One of the generals on the French side chivalrously described it as the battle of giants, but kind words couldn't change the verdict. Switzerland had to lick its wounds and take stock of its position as a small country surrounded by powerful, squabbling neighbours. The solution was neutrality—a policy as enduringly Swiss as the mountains.

During the 16th century the chronic tensions within Europe were drastically heightened by the Protestant Reformation. In 1522, five years after Martin Luther hammered home his 95 theses in Germany, a Swiss curate, Ulrich Zwingli of Zurich, challenged the pope's authority. Protestantism spread more slowly in the French-speaking region, but by 1542 the French reformer John Calvin had established a severe Protestant theocracy in Geneva. And the Bernese occupied the canton of Vaud and brought the Reformation with them. Some blood was spilled on both sides in the Reformation and Counter-Reformation.

But the Swiss stayed on the sidelines of Europe's great religious and political struggle, the Thirty Years' War. Swiss Catholics and Protestants tried to live together behind the shield of neutrality, meanwhile prospering by supplying both warring sides. When peace finally came to Europe with the treaty of Westphalia (1648), the independence of the sovereign state of Switzerland was at last universally acknowledged.

The after-shock of the French Revolution (1789) reverberated across all of Europe, not least in Switzerland. After occupying or annexing attractive slices of Swiss territory—and pushing the Bernese back to their own turf—the French set up a so-called Helvetian Republic. The Swiss abhorred its artificial, centralized structure. Three years of anarchy were put to an end by Napoleon, who gave Switzerland a new constitution (1803) based on the old Confederation, plus six new cantons including Vaud. He also imposed a heavy military levy on the Swiss and took conscripts with him to foreign fields; 8,000 Swiss died covering the emperor's retreat from Moscow.

Neutral but Caring
With the Congress of Vienna (1815) Switzerland's "perpetual neutrality" was restored. Geneva, Neuchâtel and the Valais joined the Confederation, filling out the present-day boundaries of the country. A new constitution of 1848 mapped out the grass-roots democracy still in force, with power shared by local, cantonal and federal authorities.

Switzerland's neutrality faced two harrowing tests in the 20th century—the World Wars. In each case the Swiss army and people were mobilized to defend the frontiers at any cost. In the summer of 1940 it seemed touch-and-go whether Hitler would invade, if only on general principles. The commanding general, Henri Guisan, is considered a great national hero—not for winning a war but for forging an army impressive enough to keep Switzerland out of the war.

Neutrality has propelled Switzerland to a unique position in world affairs. The special role began in 1863, when a businessman from Geneva, Henry Dunant, founded the Red Cross. (Its symbol, a red cross on a white background, is the reverse image of the flag of Switzerland.) The country has given asylum to political exiles of nearly all beliefs, from Lenin to Solzhenytsin. The League of Nations was born in Geneva, now the European headquarters of the United Nations. But Switzerland chose not to join the U.N. itself, for fear of prejudicing national neutrality.

Today, this small country stands as a model of democracy, stability and prosperity for much of the world. The Swiss now face the challenge of striking a balance between commercial interests and moral considerations, between disengagement and humanitarian principles, trying to preserve their unique assets while finding their role in the 20th century.

Red and white national flag flies through the air as twirler opens a traditional Swiss wrestling meet.

Where to Go

Although it's hemmed in by two mountain chains, the Jura and the Alps, French-speaking Switzerland has plenty of wide-open spaces. An hour's trip in any direction runs through glorious scenic contrasts: snow-topped peaks, se-mi-tropical flower gardens, timberlands and pastures, harsh gorges and dreamy lakes. But don't underestimate the towns and villages, full of charm and tradition.

Getting around is easy. You can drive on well-kept roads or use first-class public transport. Trains are fast and fantastically

punctual. Efficient bus services fill out the map. Within the cities trolley-buses and buses go everywhere swiftly. In the mountains cable-cars and funiculars, Swiss specialities, take you into the wild blue yonder. (You can walk or ski back down if you prefer.)

For convenience, French-speaking Switzerland has been divided here into segments

High above earthly cares, skiers and sightseers in cable cars float across rugged Swiss mountains. Skyline: Valais and Bernese Alps.

which don't always coincide with the cantonal boundaries. We've included a couple of daring forays across the language barrier to German-speaking Switzerland. And other excursions across the easygoing national frontier to neighbouring France.

To begin with, at the westernmost tip of Switzerland, the nation's most international city.

Geneva
Pop. 155,000

This gracious city of history and the arts, glittering shops and waterfront parks is big enough to have everything you're looking for, yet small enough to cope with. Diplomats and international functionaries hang on fiercely when threatened with a transfer. After all, Geneva has that lake, those mountains, that mild climate… and is surrounded on three sides by French cooking.

Geneva's location has been considered crucial ever since 58 B.C., when Julius Caesar and his legions rolled in. They destroyed the ancient bridge across the Rhone, right in the centre of the town, to bar Helvetian tribesmen from migrating to the south of France. Many another ruler has coveted Geneva and its strategic traffic and trade. The city has been variously controlled by the kings of Burgundy, the Holy Roman Emperor, the dukes of Savoy and, briefly, Napoleon.

In the most memorable battle for Geneva, several thousand mercenaries under the Savoyard flag attacked in 1602. They scaled the town wall at night, but the citizens, armed with anything from pikes to stewpots, sent them flying. Every December 12, Geneva celebrates L'Escalade (scaling of the walls) with a solemn but triumphant torchlight parade.

Perhaps the most improbable ruler in the town's history was the French theologian John Calvin, who made Geneva a great Protestant centre. In 1541, the citizens invited him to serve as their spiritual leader. Life became severe and dour, but Protestant refugees and pilgrims poured into the town. Today tolerance reigns. Geneva, headquarters of the World Council of Churches, is well supplied with Protestant, Catholic and Orthodox churches, plus a synagogue and a mosque.

For an overall survey of Geneva, take one of the multilingual coach tours which operate all year round. From mid-March to the end of October

excursion companies schedule boat tours every day, ranging from a half-hour look around the port to a 2½-hour survey of lakefront castles, mansions and parks.

Walking through Geneva

A logical start for a stroll is the main railway station, the Gare de Cornavin. From here it's a five-minute walk down Rue du Mont-Blanc to the lakeside—that is, if you can stay aloof from the shops and cafés lying in ambush along the way.

The tallest monument in Geneva, visible from many parts of town, is as impermanent as a summer shower. It is, in fact, a jet of water prosaically named the **Jet d'Eau.** When the wind is still, this fireman's dream is turned on, pumping lake water straight up at 500 litres per second to the height of a 40-storey building. Something like this fountain has been a trademark of Geneva's harbour for nearly a century, though the modern model is far more powerful—and more expensive to run.

The Mont-Blanc bridge is the longest and busiest one connecting the two halves of Geneva. Here you can sense a drastic change in the waterway, narrowing from a placid lake to become a surging river. The

Rhone River, born high in the Alps, flows the length of Lake Geneva until this spot, where the lake ends and the mighty river resumes its rush toward the Mediterranean.

Notice the small wooded island (man-made in the 16th century) just west of the Mont-Blanc bridge. The contem-

plative statue honours a distinguished Genevan, the philosopher Jean-Jacques Rousseau (1712–78). Behind his back is a sanctuary for swans and ducks. At feeding time all the neighbouring pigeons swoop in without invitation.

A larger island, down-river, bears the laconic name of **l'Ile**
(the island). Part of an ancient watch-tower has been preserved; a plaque quotes the historian Caesar on his visit to Geneva.

Once across the river you can

Glass façade of a modern building reflects on Geneva's Rue du Rhône.

wander up the Rue de la Corraterie, an elegant 19th-century shopping street, to the Place Neuve. Three extremely formal buildings face this spacious square: the **Grand Théâtre** (a smaller version of the Paris opera house), the Conservatoire de Musique, and the **Musée Rath,** which presents temporary art exhibits.

Behind iron gates, in the park facing Place Neuve, stands the imposing **Reformation Monument.** A long stone wall is engraved with religious texts in several languages (including 16th-century English). The major sculptural group portrays Calvin and three of his associates: the French reformers Théodore de Bèze and Guillaume Farel, and the Scottish preacher John Knox. Opposite the monument is the main building of the University of Geneva, a descendant of Calvin's theological academy.

Uphill from here is Geneva's **old town,** a well-preserved village of twisting streets, historic mansions and simple fountains lavishly embellished with flowers. Because of the strategic hilltop location, this was the area first fortified by the Romans, as you'll see from restored portions of the ancient city walls.

The highest point of the old town has been a place of worship since pagan days. The present **Cathédrale St-Pierre** (St. Peter's Cathedral) was begun in the 12th century in Romanesque style but evolved into Gothic innovation. In the 18th century the façade was remodelled, and classical columns, still controversial, were tacked on.

Of course, when it was built the cathedral was a Catholic church. Its spontaneous conversion to Protestantism occurred on Sunday, August 8, 1535, when a devout mob of Reformation enthusiasts swept into the temple and resident Catholic priests fled. Calvin preached in St-Pierre (stripped of statues, relics and images of saints) for more than 20 years.

The interior of the cathedral has recently been restored in a major reconstruction programme. The Flamboyant Gothic Chapel of the Maccabees can be reached by a separate entrance on the south side of the cathedral. You can

Monumental figures of the Reformation loom above pensive pilgrims.

24

climb to the top of the north tower, amidst the carillon bells, for a top-flight **panorama** of Geneva and vicinity.

This may include the rugged Jura mountains to the north and west and Mount Salève and even Mont-Blanc—if you're lucky—in France (see pp. 30–31).

A few steps from the cathedral, at Place de la Taconnerie, you can visit the modest chapel in which John Knox preached to English-language adherents of the new faith. The church, called the Auditoire de Calvin, was submitted to a brighter-than-new restoration programme in 1959.

Under the arcades of a building called the **Arsenal,** partly camouflaged behind flowerpots, cannon from the 17th and 18th centuries are symbolically deployed. Modern mosaics give an impression of medieval Geneva.

Geneva's **Hôtel de Ville** (town hall), across the street from the Arsenal, has an elegant Renaissance courtyard. A ramp, not a staircase, runs upstairs; visiting dignitaries could be driven all the way to their meetings at the summit. The first of the Geneva conventions on the humane treatment of prisoners-of-war was concluded in the town hall in 1864.

Soon afterwards, an international dispute growing out of the American Civil War was settled here. The historic chamber is now called, somewhat startlingly, the Salle de l'Alabama—after a Confederate warship of the same name.

The street running past the town hall turns into picturesque **Grand-Rue,** lined with buildings dating from the 15th to the 18th centuries. A plaque on the front of No. 40 indicates the house where Jean-Jacques Rousseau was born.

Back around the corner from the Hôtel de Ville, on a bluff overlooking the Promenade des Bastions, you can relax in a tree-shaded park called La Treille (the Trellis). Originally a vineyard, now a municipal park, it features what Genevans proudly call the longest park bench in the world.

International City

The elegant Quai Wilson, along the right bank of the lake, honours the 20th-century American president who profoundly affected Geneva's destiny. The city had long been a centre of book-publishing, watch-making, banking… as well as intellectual and humanitarian activities. Woodrow Wilson made it the world headquarters of diplomacy. Founding the League of Nations, he nominated Geneva as its site.

In the 60 years since that big decision, countless new international organizations and agencies have been created, and most of them seem to have set up shop in the congenial surroundings of the League's old home town. They are as diverse as the International Telecommunications Union, the International Labour Office (ILO), the General Agreement on Tariffs and Trade (GATT) and the little-heard-of World Organization for the Protection of Intellectual Property.

The spacious **Palais des Nations** was the headquarters of the League of Nations. Designed by an international committee of architects, it opened for business in 1937, when war clouds already overshadowed the League's good intentions. After World War II had run its course, the new United Nations took over the building for its European headquarters. As U. N. activities and personnel rolls inexorably multiplied, the building was further expanded, rapidly eclipsing the Palais de Versailles in acreage.

The U.N. runs half-hour guided tours. If the diplomatic heavyweights don't happen to be tussling over a treaty in closed session, you'll be taken to visit historic conference halls. You may have reservations about the architectural merit of the building, but you'll certainly like the delegates' view of the lake and the Alps.

Parks and Gardens

Geneva is rightly proud of its rich, roomy parks with their fountains, sculptures, bandstands and cafés. The highlights:

Jardin Anglais (English Garden), on the left bank, is lush and inviting. It's best known for the **flower clock**—a huge dial made up of thousands of flowers and plants changed seasonally.

Parc de la Grange features a truly sensational rose garden. Elsewhere in the park the remains of an ancient Roman villa were excavated, proving again that the Romans had good taste in real estate. **Parc des Eaux Vives,** adjoining the Grange, is beautifully landscaped.

Across the lake you'll find **Parc Mon Repos** and, next to it, **Perle du Lac** park which includes a distinguished restaurant. Inland, the **Jardin Botanique** (botanical garden) mixes beauty and erudition.

And in a mini-park on the right bank, on the Quai du Mont-Blanc, Geneva's most bizarre monument: the **tomb of the Duke of Brunswick** (1804–73). Having spent his last few years in exile in Geneva, the eccentric gentleman bequeathed the city many a worthwhile project.

Museums of Geneva

Musée d'Art et d'Histoire. Geneva's biggest and richest museum covers a lot of ground, from prehistory to modern art. An outstanding archaeological collection features local and faraway discoveries over many centuries. The most highly prized item is an altarpiece painted for St. Peter's Cathedral by Conrad Witz in 1444. Called *The Miracle of the Fishes*, it shows the Geneva countryside—the first time a European painter depicted a non-fictional background.

Musée Ariana. In a marble-columned palace surrounded by parkland, the art of ceramics unfolds from medieval Spanish pottery to modern porcelain. The park, the museum and much of the collection were donated to Geneva by a 19th-century philanthropist, Gustave Revilliod, who named the institution after his mother.

Musée de l'Horlogerie. Classic clocks tick and chime in an 18th-century mansion, Villa de Malagnou. Immensely delicate enamelled watches were a Genevan speciality.

Petit Palais. Four floors of a small palace are packed with impressionist and post-impressionist works of varying quality. Renoir and Picasso are there, but the emphasis is on lesser-known artists of the era.

Musée d'Instruments Anciens de Musique. Fritz Ernst, who collected these 300 historic musical instruments, plays some of them for visitors. He calls it the only living museum in the world. (Check unusual opening hours.)

Geneva has about a dozen more museums, including a pair devoted to the men who made the city a great 18th-century intellectual centre—Rousseau and Voltaire. In spite of their vastly differing views and styles, both authors at one time had their works banned by Geneva's ultra-righteous censor.

Note: Museum visiting hours tend to change from time to time, so it's best to consult the lists in the tourist office before setting out. Most museums, though, are open from 10 a.m. to noon and from 2 to 5 or 6 p.m. and closed on Mondays.

Carouge

Though it seems like an extension of Geneva, Carouge is a separate municipality on the south bank of the Arve River with its very own history and character. It was founded in the late 18th century by—of all unlikely powers—the King of Sardinia, who also happened to be the Duke of Savoy. In those days titles and crowns were passed around like any other family heirlooms.

The Sardinians' imperial

Assessing a rare antique, Geneva expert holds it with loving hands.

plan for Carouge was to create a serious rival to Geneva. Most of the project stayed on the drawing board, but there's no mistaking the foreignness of the town's fountains and squares, wrought-iron street-lamps and faded town-houses.

Genevans like to go to Carouge for the round-the-clock bohemian atmosphere—theatre and art and lively bars and restaurants. A colourful street market is held on Wednesday and Saturday mornings.

Foreign Affairs

Geneva is a peninsula jutting into France, so crossing the border is as commonplace as crossing town. Here are two spots the Genevans often visit on the foreign side of the rather easy-going frontier.

The Salève. This mountain is such a familiar bit of scenery for Genevans that it might as

Alpine scenes and other paintings for sale at a quaint Geneva shop.

well be a local monument. On weekends the strangely tilted cliff-face swarms with local mountain-climbers. Other intrepid sportsmen drive to the top (4,525 ft.) to practise the breathtaking art of hang-gliding. The view from the summit is superb.

Divonne. In this overgrown French village, 18 kilometres north of Geneva, you can restore your health or (much less likely) your fortune. The two principal attractions are the thermal baths and the gambling casino. Big money changes hands around the roulette, blackjack, baccarat and craps tables in an old-fashioned continental atmosphere. In summer Divonne widens its horizons with horse-racing, golf, sailing and a distinguished chamber-music festival.

Chamonix

On a very clear day you can see three-mile-high **Mont-Blanc** from the centre of Geneva, but for a close-up of Europe's highest summit you have to cross the border into France. This very popular all-day excursion takes two hours by coach from Geneva. Or you can do it yourself by car or train.

As the Matterhorn has brought fame to Zermatt, so Mont-Blanc casts its shadow and spell over the town of Chamonix. This top European winter-sports centre has the air of an Alaskan gold-rush town, with improvised architectural styles plopped together wherever a level space could be found. But the appearance of the town itself is all very secondary to the overwhelming beauty of the encircling Alps.

From Chamonix you can take one of the world's highest cable-cars above pines, stone and snow to the blinding white summit of the **Aiguille du Midi** at an altitude of 12,600 feet. At the top end of this breathtaking journey you walk across a footbridge spanning a crevasse whose depths may be invisible in snow and mist and climb to an observation station. What you see from the Aiguille du Midi depends on the weather— a head-on portrait of Mont-Blanc and unforgettable panoramas over the glacier, or perhaps nothing more than snowflakes filling a stormy sky.

Another excursion from Chamonix is by funicular to the **Mer de Glace** ("sea of ice"), where you can enter an ice-grotto and try walking around on the glacier. The trip is now very comfortable. Before the railway was built, 300 mules were employed to transport tourists to the glacier.

The Lake of Geneva

Geneva's lake—and Lausanne's, Montreux's and Evian's—is really named Léman. It has won the hearts of poets, artists, composers... and geographers and statisticians.

The largest in the Alps, about two thirds of it belongs to Switzerland, one-third to France. The lake is almost 45 miles long and up to 8½ miles wide, for an area of nearly 225 square miles.

On this mini-sea, five-foot waves can spring up suddenly. Pleasure boaters are always on the alert for perilous winds.

But much of the time it's clear sailing: a pageant of brightly striped spinnakers billowing under a pale sky cross-hatched with jet-trails; white lake-steamers manœuvering among motorboats, canoes, windsurfers and self-confident swans and ducks. Ashore, holidaymakers and locals politely vie for seats under the red parasols of outdoor cafés, where tiny glasses are filled and refilled with the local white wine—an appropriate salute to the glorious convergence here of mountains, lake and sky.

Lakeside cafés and parks offer one perspective on the Lake of Geneva and the ever-present Alps beyond. For another point of view, relax aboard an excursion boat sweeping by sunny vineyards, patrician houses and old stone villages (see p. 106). Or take the corniche road high above the lake and see how the vineyards are terraced all the way down to the gently curving shore. You can even walk all the way around the lake—given a week or two.

However you do it, try to see as many facets as possible of this unforgettable mountain lake. Even in mist and rain—not exactly a novelty in winter—the special lure of the Lake of Geneva is undeniable.

Sailing Close to the Wind

The Swiss worry about their wind currents the way the French worry about their livers. If the wind blows from the north, a cold *bise*, it's the subject of knowing conversation all day. If it's a dry, warm *föhn*, they say, you can expect headaches, stress and sometimes vertigo.

Down at the lakes, charts warn inexperienced sailors to watch for legendary local winds that might blow no good. On the Lake of Geneva, winds have names like Joran, Vent Blanc, Fraidieu, Vaudaire and Séchard. The most tempestuous of all is the French-based Bornan, which comes on at a hurricane-like 60 to 85 miles an hour.

For reasons of organization, our coverage of the lake shore's most interesting towns and landmarks begins on the eastern edge of Geneva and continues clockwise almost full circle.

La Côte

Coppet. This pleasant village of thick-walled stone houses evokes the image of Europe's 19th-century superwoman, Germaine Necker, better known as Mme de Staël. Her father, the Genevan banker Jacques Necker, bought the **château** of Coppet in 1784. A marble statue of the gentleman stands in the entrance hall.

But the point of the mansion, which is open for guided tours, is the brilliant Mme de Staël. Her portraits and memorabilia are scattered through rooms furnished in Louis XVI and Directoire style. When Napoleon exiled her from Paris, she took her intellectual salon, including the leading lights of French romanticism, along to Coppet. As one of her circle, the aristocratic philosopher Charles-Victor de Bonstetten observed: "More wit is dispensed at Coppet in one day than in the rest of the world in a year."

The château is closed on Mondays and during the winter.

Nyon. While the château of Coppet evolved into a purely residential building, the five-towered **castle** of Nyon was designed and used as a military bastion by the Savoy family. Construction began in the 12th century. In the 16th century the fortress was overpowered by troops from Berne, who then controlled the Canton of Vaud for the next 250 years.

The château's history museum presents a picture of life in medieval times. On display are a wide variety of military objects and a collection of apothecary jars. Upstairs a separate museum is devoted to examples of the porcelain produced in Nyon in the late 18th and early 19th centuries and now fiercely coveted by collectors.

Julius Caesar established an army outpost here, so that, not surprisingly, there are quite some reminders of the Romans' passage. Near the château, in rue Maupertuis, lie the remains of a Roman basilica. The ancient building, which has been enclosed, contains interesting amphoras, mosaics, coins, glass, pottery and statuary.

Another memento of the Romans: two and a half Corinthian columns, discovered under a nearby street, which have been effectively installed on the edge of a bluff at the end of the **Promenade des Vieilles Murailles** ("old walls walk"). Spread out below is a neatly gardened park and a port for both pleasure-craft and fishing boats. You may find the local anglers using a public fountain to keep a few dozen big perch alive until market time.

The fishing industry, along with historic and scientific aspects of the lake, are covered in Le Musée du Léman, a waterfront museum.

The old centre of Nyon, around the château, is a pleasure to explore: an 11th-century tower, a 12th-century church, and dozens of exemplary houses from the 15th to 19th centuries.

Rolle. Most castles were built on hilltops for strategic reasons, but the 13th-century château of Rolle, halfway between Geneva and Lausanne, is right on the lakefront. It has seen its share of fighting. The Bernese burned it twice in the 16th century.

Near the castle are pleasant lakefront promenades. Just offshore is a singular sight: a lonely artificial island. Tall trees overshadow an obelisk dedicated to Rolle's most revered citizen, Frédéric-César de La Harpe (1754–1838),

known as the father of the independence of the Canton of Vaud. At the Congress of Vienna (1814–15) he was instrumental in obtaining guarantees of the neutrality of Switzerland and the independence of Vaud and several other cantons. In an earlier career, La Harpe served as tutor to Tsar Alexander I of Russia.

Saint-Prex. In this unselfconsciously quaint medieval market town, barns and shops stand among distinguished mansions. A heavy clock tower dated 1234 surmounts the landward side of the short main street leading to the lake.

Morges. When it's tulip time in Morges you know that winter has finally been chased from the shores of the Lake of Geneva. Every April and May the Morges Tulip Festival stars more than 100 varieties of tulips—perhaps 300,000 flowers in all.

Before the railway was built, Morges had been an important port for lake freighters. It's still a nautical centre, but the boats are dinghies and yachts moored in Morges' marina by weekend sailors who live all along the coast.

Commanding the waterfront is an imposing square **château** built in the 13th century. The

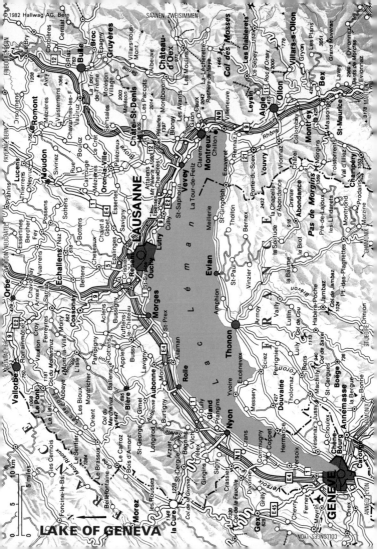

LAKE OF GENEVA

castle and the town itself were founded by Prince Louis of Savoy as a power base to rival the prince-bishop of Lausanne. Since the 19th century, parts of the building have been used as a military arsenal. In 1871 an ammunition explosion killed a score of people and broke windows as far away as Thonon, on the French side of the lake. The château now encloses the **Vaud Military Museum,** with historical costumes, battle-flags and weapons and more toy soldiers than you've ever seen—8,000 little lead figurines deployed to re-create ancient and modern battles.

Another local museum, **Musée Alexis Forel,** is a 16th-century mansion filled with valuable antique furniture and works of art.

A footnote for music-lovers. The Polish composer and statesman Ignace Paderewski lived in Morges for some years. And Igor Stravinsky composed *L'Histoire du Soldat,* in col-

The final touch and everything is ready for sailing regatta at Morges.

laboration with the Swiss author C.-F. Ramuz, in Morges in 1918.

Saint-Sulpice. The waterfront park of this quiet village is furnished with striking modern statues. There are gratifying views of the vineyards, the lake and the mountains across the way, and even an unexpected sidelong glimpse of Lausanne a few miles down the coast.

But the main reason for visiting Saint-Sulpice is a few yards inland: a touching primitive **Romanesque church.** Topped by a heavy square belfry, it was built in the 11th or 12th-century as part of a Benedictine monastery. In the 15th century the nave collapsed but the choir and transept stand by themselves as a pleasing and important architectural monument. **37**

Lausanne
Pop. 135,000

If anything's missing in Lausanne, it may be the generation gap. Cheerful coexistence links the teenager on a skateboard with the retired tycoon in a wheelchair. Old and young, tourist and native share a sense of well-being in this prosperous business, government and university centre. Something's always going on—an international music festival or an industrial exhibition or just a street-corner jazz recital.

Lausanne's mile-long lakefront, with parks and gardens, cafés and restaurants, is the liveliest, loveliest place in town when the weather's fair. More than 1,400 pleasure boats, including oceanworthy yachts, are moored in two local marinas. This is also the home port of a veritable Swiss navy of excursion ships. Watch a big white steamboat gently nudge against the wharf, letting off hordes of partying passengers. Or you can get into the swim by renting a rowing boat or a pedalo.

This part of town, called **Ouchy** (pronounced oo-shee), is not for serious sightseeing, but in your wanderings you may sight two structures of apparent importance. Right at the port, the Château d'Ouchy is a real medieval castle but it was almost totally rebuilt in the 19th century and is now a hotel. If you walk eastward to the end of the landscaped waterfront promenade, you'll be startled to see the ruins of a medieval tower. Actually it's a counterfeit, built in 1823 as a bit of a joke between local businessmen.

From Ouchy to the centre of Lausanne is too long and steep a walk to appeal to most tourists. An unusual, efficient way of going up is the grandly named Métro, a wide-bodied rack-railway train that makes the ascent in six minutes. Old-

timers still call the Métro "La Ficelle" (the string) after the original funicular built a century ago. The right-of-way alongside the track is landscaped with flowers and blooming trees. At the fourth (last) stop, called Centre Ville, take the lift up to the level of Lausanne's main traffic intersection, **Place St-François.**

This hectic square, a conglomeration of banks, shops and trolleybus stops, used to be the site of a Franciscan monastery. All that's left, on an island of peace in the middle of all this activity is the 13th-century church of **St-François.** Inside and out it's a sober work of architecture except for the 15th-century clock-tower with four turrets and a slim spire. Since 1536 it has been a Protestant church.

One of Lausanne's smartest shopping streets, the cobbled **Rue de Bourg,** wanders steeply upward from Place St-François, mostly traffic-free. If you continue climbing on Rue Caroline you'll come upon an open expanse with a first-class view of the towers of the cathedral. To get there, cross the Bessières bridge.

Only the ferry's in a hurry on a lazy day in Lausanne's port, Ouchy.

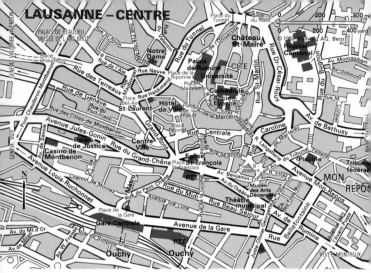

Lausanne's Gothic **cathedral** is one of the last places in the world preserving the tradition of the night watch. The night hours (10 p.m. to 2 a.m.) are called out by a watchman surveying the city from his tower.

Construction began in the 12th century. The cathedral was consecrated in 1275 at a ceremony attended by Pope Gregory X, seven cardinals, five archbishops, 17 bishops and King Rudolph of the incipient Habsburg empire.

Among remarkable 13th-century survivals in this important cathedral are a rare set of choir stalls and, almost miraculously, a **rose window.** In the fury of the Reformation almost all of the cathedral's stained-glass windows were shattered, but most of the elements of this admirable squared-circle survived. Restoration work was started in the 19th century by that eminent fixer-up of old monuments (Notre-Dame de Paris, Carcassonne) Eugène Viollet-le-Duc.

Alongside the cathedral, another historic building, the former episcopal palace, is now the **Musée Historique de l'Ancien Evêché.** Archaeological details of the town and the cathedral are on view, along with the statues of prophets and apostles which originally surrounded the south portal in the early 13th century. They have survived erosion and wear because they were painted.

Between the cathedral and the 15th-century **Château St-Maire,** now headquarters of the Vaud cantonal government, is **La Cité,** a neighbourhood

Headless Hero

Set against the south façade of the château is a monument to Major Jean-Daniel Abraham Davel (1670–1723), who challenged the canton's Bernese rulers to grant independence to Vaud. He recruited 600 soldiers and marched on Lausanne with a manifesto. He was arrested and promptly executed—decapitated in Vidy.

Unfortunately, Major Davel was 80 years ahead of his time.

Hirsute troubadour entertains the passing crowds in Rue de Bourg.

Last rays of winter sun highlight the towers of Lausanne's cathedral.

of university and government buildings and antique shops. See the panorama from the terrace between the château and the building of the Grand Conseil (cantonal legislature)—the best sunsets in town!

Covered staircases lead from the cathedral to **Place de la Palud,** Lausanne's marketplace since medieval times. On Wednesday and Saturday mornings the entire area becomes an irresistible street market—flowers, temptingly arranged vegetables and fruits, country bread and cakes. This does not detract from the dignity of Lausanne's 17th-century **Hôtel de Ville** (city hall), with its arches, capricious clocktower and fierce gargoyles. The fountain in the square portrays Justice as a good-looking woman showing a bit more leg than is usual on these occasions. It is a 20th-century replica of a 16th-century statue.

The Saturday flea market centres on Place de la Riponne, Lausanne's biggest square. As you would expect in an overdeveloped country, the junk is very high class and nothing is very cheap. But you'll enjoy roaming among the displays of antiques, clothes, jewellery and slightly read books.

Lausanne Museums

Riponne's overblown Palais de Rumine, in "Florentine Renaissance" style from the turn of the present century, is big enough to contain several museums. The **Musée Cantonal des Beaux-Arts** (Fine Arts Museum) is strong on Swiss artists. The archaeological department of the museum

42

gives pride of place to a 22-carat gold likeness of the Roman emperor Marcus Aurelius (A.D. 121–180) affecting a very contemporary haircut and beard. The $3^{1}/_{2}$-pound bust was discovered at Avenches (see pp. 78, 80).

La Collection d'Art Brut, in a converted château near the Palais de Beaulieu convention centre, is quite possibly the most original, haunting museum in Switzerland. *Art brut* (literally raw art) is sometimes translated as "outsiders' art". Each artist displayed here has *invented* his or her own school of art, and often the implements and medium as well. The results are quite astonishing flights of genius by untrained talents, some of them mentally unbalanced. The psychological history of each artist is posted along with more conventional biographical details (in French only). This 5,000-piece collection was founded by the French artist Jean Dubuffet.

The **Musée Romain de Vidy,** near the site of a 15th-century leper colony at Maladière, displays old Roman statuary and inscriptions unearthed in the surrounding area. Of unusual value is a collection of 72 Roman gold coins that were amassed by a Roman numismatist of the 2nd century A.D.

On the other side of the *auto-route,* near the lakefront, was the original Roman settlement of Lousonna. The layout of the ancient town's centre is clearly visible in the foundations of the

Imagination unleashed: "raw art" on view in Collection d'Art Brut.

buildings in the Vidy archaeological zone. The ruins have been preserved and tidied in Swiss style.

By coincidence, the definitive history of Rome was written in Lausanne. Edward Gibbon (1737–94) finished his *History of the Decline and Fall of the Roman Empire* during the years he spent as a houseguest around the corner from Place St-François. Like the empire, Gibbon's house has fallen.

Parlez-Vous Suisse?
Your school French will serve you well in Suisse Romande, though local accents and intonations may sound a bit odd. Some Swiss words differ from the classic French. In many towns, they say *syndic*, for example, instead of *maire* for mayor; *septante*, *huitante* and *nonante* are the usual words in these parts for seventy, eighty and ninety; and you're likely to hear people referring to breakfast as *déjeuner*, the midday meal as *dîner* and evening eating as *souper*.

Academics in Neuchâtel are compiling a dictionary of the many local *patois* (unofficial dialects) of French-speaking Switzerland. At last report, they had put together 3,800 pages and were only up to the letter "e".

Vaud Riviera

Sprawling in the sun from the outskirts of Lausanne to the eastern end of the Lake of Geneva, the Vaud Riviera is a land of sophisticated resorts and one-industry villages pervaded by the musty smell of wine. You never know what to expect around the next turn in the road—a flower garden, a wine press, a chalet or a château. But you'll almost always be surrounded by steep vineyards which produce the heady Lavaux wine.

No matter how you travel the views are superb—by boat looking up at the golden hillsides; by train right along the coast; by car on the coast road or the panoramic **Route du Vignoble** (route of the vineyards) or the utilitarian but spectacular *autoroute*.

Towns and villages along the way that rate a glance or a stroll:

Lutry. An unspoiled lakefront town with a Gothic church retaining some original Romanesque details, a château built by the Bernese, and a wine industry humming efficiently unseen in cellars beneath the old stone houses. They hold a rousing wine festival here in October.

Epesses. A typical wine- **45**

growing village with old stone houses and narrow, steep streets; noted for its fine white wine.

Saint-Saphorin. A totally delightful old village of flowered lanes with a 16th-century church and an esteemed (and expensive) local wine.

Vevey

Wine and milk-chocolate keep this lakeside town afloat. The biggest building in Vevey, a curved-glass structure in United Nations style, is the world headquarters of Nestlé, the multinational food company. As for wine, the Romans of 2,000 years ago were probably the first to plant grapes on the local hillsides. The importance of wine has been celebrated about once every 25 years since the 18th century in Vevey's Fête des Vignerons (winegrowers' festival), one of Europe's biggest and happiest folk manifestations (last one held in 1977).

The wine pageant and most other events in Vevey centre on the **Grande Place,** the town's disproportionately big square. On any Saturday it becomes a real country market with a rich mixture of essentials and trivialities on sale: home-baked pastries, slightly outdated fashions, the freshest flowers... or a used fireman's helmet. On his way to Italy, Napoleon reviewed his troops in the Grande Place. Many another foreigner has valued Vevey's more peaceful attractions: Dostoevsky, Gogol, Victor Hugo, Saint-Saëns, Paderewski, Wagner.

Between the lake and the railway station, old Vevey is a walkable district of 18th- and 19th-century houses, often flying traditional emblems which identify shops or cafés.

The **Musée du Vieux-Vevey,** in a lakefront château, shows how things have changed since early times. Another local museum, the **Musée Jenisch,** specializes in Swiss painting of the 19th and 20th centuries.

Above the railway line, surrounded by chestnut trees, stands Vevey's oldest church, **St-Martin.** Its 15th-century tower looks like a compromise between a cathedral and a castle. Actually, it once had a spire that was blown over by freak storms.

A rack-railway takes you from Vevey to **Les Pléiades,** a

Pitching in to gather the grapes in the Lavaux region in October.

47

belvedere more than 4,500 feet above sea level, with views of the lush landscape down to the lake and across to the French Alps. About halfway up is **Blonay,** with a 12th-century château and a nostalgic tourist railway equipped with turn-of-the-century locomotives and passenger carriages. Steam's up every Saturday and Sunday from May to the end of October on the Blonay-Chamby choo-choo.

From vineyards and orchards above Vevey a funicular climbs to another vantage point, **Mont-Pèlerin,** in a region of woods, farms, villas and sweeping vistas.

Montreux

The lake has narrowed, and the mountains ascending steeply behind Montreux shield the town from north winds. A 3-mile **lakeside promenade** exploits this unique hothouse atmosphere: all kinds of flowers thrive here and even palm trees stand firm on this alien shore.

This is a full-time, big-time tourist resort, where large old-fashioned hotels and a few new ones cater to the cosmopolitan visitor's every whim. The service and the view are so special that novelist Vladimir Nabokov chose to live permanently in his Montreux hotel suite.

The old-world look of the

Steam railway enthusiasts attend to smallest details for authenticity on the nostalgic Blonay-Chamby line.

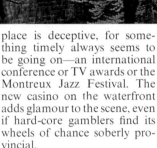

place is deceptive, for something timely always seems to be going on—an international conference or TV awards or the Montreux Jazz Festival. The new casino on the waterfront adds glamour to the scene, even if hard-core gamblers find its wheels of chance soberly provincial.

Up the hill behind the lakeside glitter is the **old town** with its 18th-century stone houses, chalets, wrought-iron balconies, antique and artisan shops, galleries and huge barns. At the top is the **Temple St-Vincent**, now a Protestant church. A recent renovation successfully melded the 12th- and 15th-century architecture with daringly modern stained-glass windows.

Montreux is a springboard for train trips to ski resorts as famous as Gstaad. Another mountain railway goes up to **Caux,** a balcony over Lake Geneva, and on to **Rochers-de-Naye,** a 6,700-foot summit with an all-round spectacular view and a nearby alpine garden with hundreds of varieties of delicate mountain flowers that bloom in early summer. **49**

Château de Chillon

Switzerland's best-known castle, Chillon is a moody feudal fortress which has known battles and torture, feasts and romance. Its turrets and towers have survived centuries of upheavals and even today they survive the tremor and roar of express trains hurtling past the door. It could have been worse. The 19th-century railway builders wanted to tear down the château and use the historic stones to prop up their right-of-way.

Some fortifications must have been right on this spot since ancient times; the great rock of Chillon, projecting

from the lake, was a natural strongpoint guarding the highway between Rome and its northern empires.

A rudimentary castle, belonging to the bishops of Sion, was greatly strengthened and expanded under the 13th-century counts of Savoy, based on the opposite shore of the lake.

In 1536, after a three-day siege by land and lake, the fortress fell to the Bernese.

Nobody welcomed the conquerers to Chillon with more sincere gratitude than François

Montreux's sedate old reputation gets a shake-up when participants arrive for its great jazz festival.

de Bonivard, a Genevan activist with influential enemies among the Catholic Savoyards. Before his liberation he had spent six years as a prisoner in the château, the last four chained to a pillar. A couple of centuries later Rousseau wrote briefly about Bonivard's suffering. Lord Byron, touring the lake with Shelley, heard the story in 1816. Generations of schoolchildren, studying Byron's first-person narrative in "The Prisoner of Chillon", may have thought it was the poet himself doing time inside "Chillon's snow-white battlement".

Visitors to the château are shown Bonivard's pillar and the channels his footsteps wore into the stone floor. But he was luckier than many prisoners in this period when all manner of atrocities were common.

Medieval stronghold of Chillon is Switzerland's most popular castle.

But you needn't be wary about crossing the moat to this treasured stronghold. Aside from a few spooky corners, Chillon leaves a sunny impression of festive banquet halls and flowered courtyards and alpine views.

Across the Lake

Continuing clockwise around the shore, beyond the point where the Rhone enters the Lake of Geneva, we reach the Swiss-French frontier at SAINT-GINGOLPH. The border is a small stream rushing down from the Savoy Alps, right through the middle of town. Townsfolk walk back and forth freely, presumably buying milk on the Swiss side and bread in France. Swiss customs men in grey uniforms and their French counterparts in blue wave foreign tourists on foot through with virtually no formalities.

Evian-les-Bains. Directly across the lake from Lausanne, this is a French festival and convention centre, resort and spa. Drinking great quantities of the local mineral water is believed to benefit kidney disorders, among others, so sufferers have long come to Evian to "take the cure". Bottles of the famous water are sold everywhere in France, but in Evian it also gushes out of the hillside.

Flowery promenades, a beach, a yacht harbour, luxury hotels and a big old-fashioned casino fill the Evian waterfront. Swiss gamblers, deprived of French roulette and chemin-de-fer on their own soil, commute from Lausanne by steamer (35 minutes).

Thonon-les-Bains. A pretty little port greets passengers arriving on excursion boats. But the town itself is on a terrace 180 feet above the lake, with gardens and excellent perspectives over the lake, the Swiss shore and the Jura mountains. Considerably larger than Evian, Thonon is also a spa. A couple of miles east, along the shore, the **Château de Ripaille** is surrounded by forests. In the 14th century it was the favourite country home of the dukes of Savoy.

Yvoire. Here the lake narrows, dividing the big eastern crescent of the Grand-Lac from the Petit-Lac. Yvoire is an endearing village of fishermen and artisans. It has a medieval castle and ramparts and a profusion of flowers.

Hermance. Back across the border in Switzerland, you'll find a relaxed medieval town with 13th-century defences and lots of waterfront space for camping, swimming and boating.

53

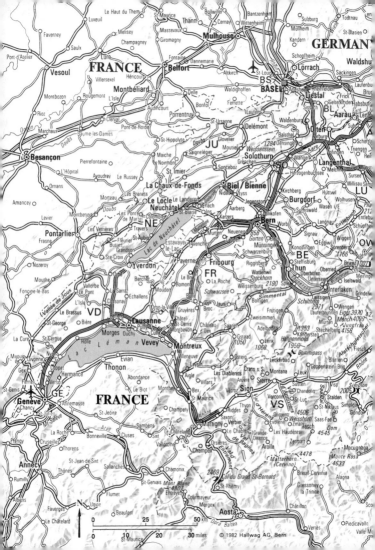

The Valais

Nature grabs your imagination in the Valais: thin waterfalls plunging down sheer mountainsides; blinding white glaciers and flowering orchards; cowbells clanging across pastures so high you'll have to catch your breath.

The Valais skyline, at times menacingly close, consists of some of the highest peaks in the Alps. Between them, from the Rhone Glacier to the shore of Lake Geneva, the lifeline of the Valais is the meandering Rhone River. Before history was recorded, this valley was the main route between north and south Europe. Now the highway and railway alongside the river bring international tourists to the canton's 100 aerial cableways and 350 ski-lifts.

The high Alps block out the cold winds and much of the rain, giving the valleys a mellow dry climate conducive to raising fruit and wine and to leisure pursuits. Each side valley is different from the next, with its own costumes and traditions. Halfway through the canton the language suddenly changes from French to Swiss-German. Almost before you can say "*merci*" someone is answering "*bitte*". What keeps the Valais united despite the linguistic division is the predominance of the Catholic religion. This is a land of historic churches as well as those storied mountain monks.

Saint-Maurice. Crammed between a precipitous cliff and a range of less hostile mountains, this town may not appeal to the claustrophobic. But it is a precious storehouse of religion and art.

The **Abbaye de St-Maurice** is one of the oldest monastic institutions in Christendom. Relays of monks, later canons, have been singing psalms here for perhaps 14 centuries. All this fervour commemorates a Roman army officer, Maurice, whose conscience kept him from obeying orders. Because he refused to kill fellow Christians, Maurice and his followers in the Theban Legion were massacred here.

Since the dark ages pilgrims have been coming to this spot to leave simple offerings and gold and silver at the tomb of the martyrs. This is the **treasure** now locked behind three high-security doors inside the basilica of St-Maurice. A taped commentary describes the pieces of greatest rarity, beginning with three large reliquaries in glass cases in the middle of the vault. The 12th-century *Head* *of St. Candidus,* an embossed silver bust, would be a prize for any museum in the world. But the oldest item in this treasure-house is the **Sardonyx Vase,** an exquisitely carved pre-Christian container onto which gold and precious stones were added in the 7th century.

Because of the small area of the vault and a lack of supervisory personnel, a limited number of visitors can be accommodated inside the treasury. Telephone in advance (025) 651181 to be sure of seeing this collection.

Martigny. The Rhone makes a brisk right-angle turn at Martigny, a crossroad town of significance since ancient times. The Roman amphitheatre (now a ruin) had seats for 6,000 spectators. On a stark hillock overlooking the town the gloomy tower of a 13th-century château has been restored. You may want to visit the Fondation Pierre-Gianadda, a museum of Roman antiquities and a cultural centre sponsoring musical events and temporary exhibits.

Grand-St-Bernard. Travellers in a hurry take the tunnel linking Switzerland and Italy, 4 miles long. Opened in 1964, it cuts beneath the worst hazards of the Great St. Bernard Pass, the classic route across the Alps at more than 8,000 feet. The new road also misses the famous **hospice** founded around 1045 by St. Bernard of Menthon. If you have time to make the detour, visit the chapel with its rich 17th-century pulpit and stalls and the historical museum. At the kennels behind the hotel you can see the lovable brown-and-white dogs that used to ferret avalanche victims out of the snow. The dogs and the monks who worked with them maintained a tradition of rescue for more than nine centuries.

Sion

The landscape here is simply fantastic: the Alps all around, the Rhone minding its own business, and suddenly two grotesque humps popping up from the valley floor. Each of these natural sites had its own medieval citadel.

Nearly 1,000 years ago Sion added political and religious authority to its military significance. The bishops of Sion were given sweeping powers over the people of their realm, meaning all of the Valais. The best-remembered of the bishops, Cardinal Matthew Schiner (1465–1522), is a national hero notwithstanding his wheeling and dealing and occasional errors of judgment.

Starting with the hills of Sion: Tourbillon, on the left, is crowned with the ruins of a 13th-century castle. Valère, on the right, supports a formidable fortress-church. You don't need mountain-climbing ability to reach the summit of either hill, but if you only have the energy for one of them, choose **Valère.** There is much to see in the Romanesque and Gothic church, formerly cathedral of Sion: naïve stone carvings, 15th-century frescoes,

and 17th-century choir-stalls. Finally, a superlative: the organ in this church is the oldest playable organ in the world. Built in 1395, it is still used for concerts (every summer). The rest of the church compound, about 35 rooms rambling down the hillside, is now a museum. Look for rare religious relics as well as prosaic old farm tools, costumes and crossbows.

At the foot of the hills, in Rue des Châteaux, are two more museums. The museum of **La Majorie,** formerly the residence of church officials, shows paintings of Sion and the people of the Valais. Across the street, the modern **archaeological museum** (Musée d'Archéologie) starts with prehistoric gravestones and works up to Roman relics.

Down in the town itself, see the 17th-century town hall, painted pink. The **cathedral** (Notre-Dame du Glarier) is a late-Gothic structure attached to a Romanesque belfry.

Finally to the **Maison Supersaxo** just off Supersaxo Street. Supersaxo? Jörg auf der Flüe, who changed his name to the Latin Georgius Supersaxo, was

Exquisite 12th-century head glows in St-Maurice; traditional painted house in Les Haudères, Valais.

an important character in the 16th-century Valais history who spent most of his life fighting with Cardinal Schiner. Father of 23 children, Supersaxo built this mansion mostly to flash his wealth in the face of the cardinal. The sculpted ceilings are admirably overdone.

Sion is a good starting point for excursions into the mountains on both sides. Off to the north, you'll find the sunny ski centre of Montana/Crans (see p. 65) and Anzère, a modern resort. On the south side, the **Val d'Hérens** is noted for its picturesque villages with dark wooden chalets generously adorned in summer with red geraniums. In the area around Évolène the women wear their traditional black-skirted costumes to work in the fields.

At the end of the Val d'Hérémence looms Europe's tallest dam, **La Grande-Dixence.** Nearly a mile and a half above sea level, this is a triumph of engineering amidst stunning scenery. A wall 930 feet high retains 14 billion cubic feet of water. The point of it all is to produce clean, cheap electricity on a massive scale. One more statistical curiosity: 200 million cubic feet of concrete were poured into the dam, enough, it's said, to build two great pyramids of Egypt.

Sierre. In this last bastion of the French language heading east along the Rhone, you'll see signs indicating: "Sierre/Siders". Local boosters point out that Sierre is the only town in Switzerland entirely surrounded by vineyards. There are ample facilities for sampling the product. With an average annual rainfall of barely 10 inches, Sierre can almost guarantee visitors a sunny stay.

Splendid sidetrips can be made up into the **Val d'Anniviers,** which claims to have Europe's highest year-round inhabited village, Chandolin (6,350 ft.) as well as a number of other charming mountain resorts such as St-Luc, Grimentz and Zinal at the foot of the Weisshorn. On the other side of Sierre is **Leuk** (Loèche), a town with a marvellous view and a good number of historic châteaux and towers dating from the time when officials of the bishops of Sion lived here, and the spa of **Leukerbad** (Loèche-les-Bains), a major centre for hiking and mountain climbing and the end point of the popular Alpine crossing of the Gemmi pass.

Getting around in car-free Zermatt: skiers await next stage-coach.

Zermatt

This mile-high, year-round ski resort takes its fresh air seriously; the nearest car is five kilometres away. Local transport includes a fleet of horse-drawn sleighs, carriages and stage-coaches—radio dispatched! So goes Zermatt's happy combination of old-

Valais Cow-fights

No, not bull-fights. Cow-fights. Cow versus cow. Very special cows, as big as Spanish fighting bulls, specially bred for pugnacity and shrewdness. It's known as the battle of the queens, *combat des reines*. Horn to horn, chests heaving, tendons rippling, they stay locked in combat until the weaker turns tail. The brighter animals seem to use psychological warfare so that the opponent is simply... cowed.

In the Valais, the dark brown fighting cows and their fans are swept up in a sort of madness on Sundays in springtime. The cows, just freed from their winter barns, thrill to the prospect of alpine pasture. The spectators squat on a hillside, swigging white wine from the bottle and arguing about the chances of Coucou against Lisette, of Mignonne against Farouk. With a couple of hundred cowbells clanging all at once the place sounds like New Year's eve in a village full of churches.

Aspects of the Valais: courtyard of 17th-century Stockalper Castle in Brig; aggressive cows tête-à-tête; farmer decked out for folklore fête. **63**

fashioned charm and new-fangled comfort and convenience.

All day long Zermatt lives under the spell of the **Matterhorn,** altitude 14,688 feet, with its history full of drama, triumph and tragedy. The peak's transcendental, mystical power is earnestly respected in the town. Its famous silhouette resembles a sea-lion poised to balance a ball on its nose.

The Matterhorn still claims about a dozen lives each year. But, then, as many as 60 climbers challenge the mountain on any summer day. A perilous undertaking, even if you're experienced, in good condition and have the professional assistance of a local guide!

Sedentary tourists can take the cog railway up to Gornergrat for a close look at the Matterhorn and a fabulous mountain-top vista. Europe's highest cableway goes up to the Little Matterhorn (12,533 feet).

Although Zermatt is in the Swiss-German-speaking area of Valais, people from Basel or Berne are baffled by the local dialect—spoken too fast for an outsider to catch. In practice, conventional German, French and English are used in hotels, restaurants and ski-schools. All mountain towns tend to be tightly knit communities. Zermatt, an extreme example, is run by a closed corporation of citizens formally called the Bourgeoisie. Only one "foreign" family has penetrated this mountain "mafia" since 1618. While many outsiders are allowed to live and work in Zermatt, only the descendants of the original 185 families belong to the official Bourgeoisie, which owns the forests, mountains and hotels.

When the first foreigners—a botanical and geological expedition—arrived in Zermatt two centuries ago they were met with a mixture of terror and hostility. The deeply religious villagers still try to shield their youngsters from the frenzy of après-ski hedonism. But they no longer stare at the jet-setters with their garish costumes and customs. They know you can't stop progress.

Brig

Other Swiss towns may have mixed feelings about Napoleon but Brig named a street after him. It salutes the military genius who built the Simplon route across the Alps, which begins here.

For many travellers Brig is just a place to change trains or fuel the car (the town has enough filling stations for a metropolis). But three buildings here are of considerably more than passing interest.

In this town of towers and turrets, the three exotic domes of the **Stockalper Castle** stand out. Baron Kaspar Jodok von Stockalper (1601–90), the most successful businessman in Valais history, built it as ostentatiously as possible. It was the biggest private house in Switzerland, with a nine-storey tower and an arcaded courtyard big enough to serve as the warehouse for the transalpine shipping service, one of Stockalper's monopolies. Today the building is the seat of local government, but visitors are taken through the formal and family rooms. A regional museum on the premises stresses Valais crafts and customs.

Nearby, the Brig parish church provides a startling contrast to Stockalper's presumptious project. Inside a simple modern (1970) building, the white altarpiece beneath a black tent-like ceiling is dazzlingly effective.

One kilometre west of Brig, a 16th-century clock tower announces an unexpectedly big and ornate **church** in the suburb of GLIS. It has an opulent gold triptych and other skilfully wrought Gothic and Renaissance features.

Top Alpine Resorts

The following is an alphabetical rundown of ten internationally known mountain resorts in this area—ski spots in winter, hiking and mountaineering bases in summer. The highest offer summer skiing as well. Three of our arbitrary ten are in German-speaking Switzerland, where the peaks are often taller.

Champéry (alt. 3,450 ft.): A front-line outpost of the "ski-without-frontiers" region, where skiing over to France adds glamour to the exercise. Neighbouring French (Avoriaz) and Swiss (Les Crosets) resorts pool their 180 ski-lifts and over 500 kilometres of marked ski-runs. Otherwise, skating, curling, tennis, swimming with the Dents du Midi mountains for company.

Château d'Oex (pronounced Chateau DAY; alt. 3,140 ft.): More homey than exotic, but appealing no less in a wide, welcoming valley. Two aerial cableways and ten ski-lifts, some downhill runs reserved for ski-bobs, plus first-rate cross-country trails. In spring the hillsides are white with narcissus instead of snow.

Crans/Montana (alt. 4,900 ft.): Actually five towns combining forces to make up Switzerland's biggest ski area—room

as the dozing cows. This small, family-style resort is near the aerial cableway up to the top of the Diablerets Glacier (9,700 ft.). The trip to the top, in three exciting stages, takes half an hour. Year-round skiing at the higher levels. Good cross-country trails around Les Diablerets.

Gstaad (alt. 3,450 ft.): This pretty town in the Bernese Oberland is as relaxed, informal and self-confident as the owner of a yacht. The social life, scenery and skiing attract a clientele of celebrities. But ordinary holidaymakers can enjoy the same 24 cableways, 28 lifts and 150 kilometres of downhill runs and a wide variety of cross-country trails. In summer, swimming, golf, tennis, horseback-riding, clay-pigeon shooting, fishing and the Menuhin music festival.

Leysin (alt. 4,100 ft.): On a steep, spectacular, sunny site facing the Dents du Midi, Leysin offers easy and intermediate skiing but energetic après-ski activity. Quite a sports centre in other respects, too—ice-skating, curling, swimming, tennis, and that most Swiss of pursuits, archery.

for 4,500 guests in hotels and 20,000 more in chalets and apartments. Ten cableways and 25 ski-lifts go as high as 9,800 feet where you can lunch in a modern restaurant before skiing "home". This sunny spot is well known for its nightlife and good restaurants. Après-ski fans will find Crans more chic than Montana. In summer, golf and tennis.

Les Diablerets (alt. 3,800 ft.): Chalets are arranged on the

66 hillsides here as spontaneously

Winter sun and merry spirits add to popularity of Swiss resorts; ski trails carve hieroglyphs in snow.

Saas-Fee (alt. 5,900 ft.): Beneath the Fee glacier, the town's name is probably derived from the German *Vieh* (livestock) and not the more fetching word *Fee* (fairy). This resort, surrounded by giant peaks, has lifts up to 10,000 feet for year-round skiing. Until 1951 the village could only be reached by mule-train, a five-hour trek. Cars are still, mercifully, banned inside the town.

Verbier (alt. 4,920 ft.): 150 kilometres of slopes for all grades of skiers, from professionals to four-year-olds. The sunny Alpine village atmosphere remains amidst the new skyscrapers; the townsfolk seem unaffected by the après-ski elegance including mink-coated beauties in "moon boots", fur mukluks.

Villars (alt. 4,110 ft.): Cheerful chalets and apartment-blocks in chalet form amidst the pines. Villars offers a wide choice of ski lifts and a train up to Bretaye, 50 kilometres of signposted downhill runs plus cross-country trails. A family resort, but no shortage of discos and bars.

Zermatt (alt. 5,300 ft.): The inescapable influence over this fashionable resort is the Matterhorn, a jagged tooth of stone nearly three miles high. As for skiing, one "underground",

68

36 cablecars and skilifts and 150 kilometres of downhill runs for all levels of skiers from as high as 12,533 feet. Fanatics enjoy year-round skiing by helicopter. No cars allowed. See also pp. 61, 64.

The Swiss Jura

Rubbing high shoulders with France, this sparsely settled border region contrasts rugged cliffs, verdant pastures and mountain lakes mirroring pine forests. Life is harsh in this corner of the world, where watch-making has been a vital cottage industry for centuries. Suddenly Switzerland looks less plump and prosperous here, the houses a bit drab and faded from countless ravaging winters. But for the tourist in search of peace and beauty, the Jura is a major discovery.

Romainmôtier. This simple village, in a little valley all its own, takes its name from the monastery (*moutier* in Old French) founded here around the year 450 by St. Romain. The present church, the third on the site, was built in the 10th and 11th centuries. It is far too small to be a cathedral but quite as majestic.

The outlines of two earlier churches are still visible in the floor near the organ. Look for the 12th- and 13th-century frescoes and the Romanesque sculptures of medieval horrors and marvels. The rarest piece of carved stone is the 7th-century ambo (early Christian pulpit), discovered in recent excavations.

In 1536 the church came under the control of the Reformation forces from Berne. Catholic statues and paintings were removed or destroyed, and the monastery closed up. Romainmôtier has been a Protestant church ever since.

Vallorbe. For rail travellers on the main line from Paris to Milan, Vallorbe is the first stop in Switzerland. It may seem to consist entirely of customs men and railway officials.

A few miles to the southwest, where the River Orbe emerges, is the entrance to **Les Grottes de Vallorbe** (the Vallorbe caves). A 50-minute guided tour leads you through the chill world of stalactites, stalagmites, subterranean torrents and mysterious lagoons.

La Chaux-de-Fonds. After a fire wiped out the town in the late 18th century, it was rebuilt in a strict grid pattern, with avenues and streets chopped into rectangular blocks. On a map it looks rather like Manhattan. On the ground it's definitely Switzerland, with the Jura rising right behind the town.

The most famous son of La Chaux-de-Fonds was Charles-Edouard Jeanneret (1887–1965). We know him as Le Corbusier, the architect who put us all into efficient, reinforced concrete buildings. He probably wouldn't have fancied the 22-storey "skyscraper" now hanging above the business district.

In La Chaux-de-Fonds more than most places, time is money. The industrial base for this town of nearly 40,000 inhabitants is watchmaking. By no coincidence the best museum here—and one of the best in Switzerland—is the **Musée International d'Horlogerie** (Rue des Musées 29). The fascinating exhibit begins with sundials and sand-clocks and works its way up to the most modern chronometers. You can watch technicians restoring antique clocks and watches, and see examples of the latest Swiss efforts to keep ahead of the competition in technology. (If you're interested in visiting a major watch factory, it's best to organize this in advance by writing to the local tourist office.)

Next door to the watch museum is the town's fine-arts museum *(Musée des Beaux-* **69**

Arts), where you will discover that Le Corbusier was an artist as well as an architect.

Saint-Ursanne. The rushing River Doubs arrives from France, makes a hairpin turn around a timbered hill and— *voilà!*—as appealing a hamlet as you'll ever see. Saint-Ursanne's pink, ochre and white stone houses, some of them quite tipsy with age, crowd against the river bank. Under the humpbacked one-lane bridge, kingfishers dart above the water like nervous helicopters. Old men in black berets bask in the sunshine alongside the 12th-century Eglise Collégiale. The church, with its intriguing Romanesque sculptural work, and the village itself are named after Ursicinus, a wandering Irishman of the 7th century. He achieved his saintliness as a hermit alongside the River Doubs.

Porrentruy. Halfway between La Chaux-de-Fonds and Basel, the Swiss border makes

Dr Jean Chausse, La Neuveville

an arrow-shaped incursion into France. At the centre of this hilly peninsula is Porrentruy, a town with an unlikely story. In 1527, when the Reformation arrived in Basel, the Prince-Bishop retreated to Porrentruy. For two-and-a-half centuries this small Jura town was a considerable religious and political capital and many of the buildings attest to this stature. The medieval red-roofed **château,** with a couple of onion domes for variety, was the headquarters of the prince-bishopric. The town hall and other 18th-century official buildings are especially well executed. All the houses with wrought-iron balconies and shuttered windows of unexpected sizes and shapes make Porrentruy look more French than Swiss and more princely than most towns of 7,000 souls.

Jura landscape: watch-making in homesteads, horsebreeding outside.

Three Lakes

On a fertile plateau paralleling the Jura mountains, three linked lakes are a focus of recreation and history. Lake Neuchâtel is Switzerland's biggest "interior" lake—that is, not bordering another country. The two other interconnected lakes amount to a statistical drop in the bucket; all three together would fill less than half the area of the Lake of Geneva.

Switzerland's capricious linguistic frontier runs along the banks of all three lakes. Two of them are known by double names: Bienne/Biel and Morat/Murten. It may seem ironic—or is it defiant?—but they claim that the purest French in Switzerland is spoken in the metropolis of this borderland, Neuchâtel.

Lake of Neuchâtel

Neuchâtel's lake is large enough to accommodate serious regattas, roomy excursion steamers and millions of fish. Because it's set on an open plain, the lake can become tempestuous when stormy winds blow.

Strange historical tides have washed across Neuchâtel. It belonged to such varied rulers as the Holy Roman Emperor, the dukes of Burgundy and the kings of Prussia. (Not until the mid-19th century did Prussia go through the formalities of setting Neuchâtel free—more than 40 years after it had joined the Swiss confederation.)

The town of **Neuchâtel** (pop. 36,000) is a centre of scientific research for the watch industry. The beep-beep-beep of the official Swiss time signal originates at the observatory here. The university and specialized schools and institutes carry on a long intellectual tradition. Finally, the lake generates tourism. The compact port of Neuchâtel shelters excursion boats, yachts, sailing boats and pedalos.

The old crossroads of the town, the Croix-du-Marché, is only a few streets inland. Here the buildings and fountains date from the 16th to 18th centuries. The most original construction is the **Maison des Halles,** designed as a covered market, with fine Renaissance decorations. In this lively part of town you can mingle with shoppers at the street market or watch the hurly-burly from the sidelines at a café table.

At the top of the town is a monumental medieval complex which neatly blurred the line dividing church and state. Church, prison and government headquarters were all mingled behind common defences. The great 13th-century church, **La Collégiale,** had its name and denomination changed with the Reformation in 1530. Inside, a remarkable 14th–15th-century sculptural group immortalizes the counts of Neuchâtel. The bleak ancient architecture of the cloister is eased by ivy, grass and flowers.

The 12th–16th-century **château** is built of the same mustard-coloured stone as the church. The romance of the medieval court of honour of the château may waver a bit when you notice the list of its present inhabitants—such as the cantonal departments of finance and public works. The best vantage point over the town and the lake is the top of the 15th-century **prison tower** *(Tour des Prisons) . . .* if you don't mind the 125 wooden steps.

Further on, in the **Musée d'Ethnographie** (Rue St-Nicolas 2–4), you can see fine, extremely well-presented collections from Ancient Egypt, Africa and Oceania.

Neuchâtel's two most important museums share a building at the port. The **Musée des Beaux-Arts** (fine arts) exhibits Swiss artists and medieval religious paintings. The **Musée d'Histoire** (history) is a catch-all of rare Swiss ceramics, 16th-century pocket-watches, assorted armour, coins and medals. Best of all are three androids—robots in human form—made by the 18th-century Swiss clockmaker Pierre Jaquet-Droz. Called the *Musician,* the *Draughtsman* and the *Writer,* they move with seemingly human grace. On the first Sunday of each month from 2.30 to 4 p.m. the automatons give a public "concert".

Grandson, now a town of 2,000 inhabitants, was the scene of one of the greatest triumphs in Swiss history. In 1476 the Duke of Burgundy, Charles the Bold, was defeated here by gallant Confederate troops from Berne and Central Switzerland. For a vivid description of the event, see the toy-soldier layouts and abandoned Burgundian battle flags and weapons, on show in Grandson's five-towered **château.** The castle was built in the 13th century on foundations laid about the year 1,000. You can explore the ramparts, joined by a shaky, authentic wooden walkway. An interesting antique car museum shares the premises.

Grandson's other treasure is the **Eglise St-Jean-Baptiste** (St. John the Baptist), a Ro-

manesque church begun in the 11th or 12th century. Spotlights can be turned on to bring into focus the religious and fantasy themes carved atop the stone columns of the nave.

Yverdon-les-Bains. The statue in front of the town hall—a man talking to two children—is of Pestalozzi (1746–1827), a pioneer of pedagogy. Zurich-born, he ran an institute in Yverdon's **château** for 20 years. The municipal museum, in the same 13th-century castle, devotes a room to him. It also covers a lot of ground from cave-man relics to primitive bicycles, with a couple of Egyptian mummies thrown in.

Since Roman times Yverdon has been known for its mineral baths, which are flourishing anew. The sulphur content of the water is said to be useful in the treatment of rheumatism and other maladies. The town (pop. about 20,000) has a horse-racing season twice a year.

Estavayer-le-Lac. All manner of architecture stands side by side in this old walled town, from thick arcaded ground floors to delicate stonework and carved doors. The 13th-

century Château de Chenaux, with circular red-brick towers, once belonged to the dukes of Savoy and now serves as headquarters for the local police force. The church in the centre of town *(St-Laurent)* is mostly late Gothic. Estavayer's museum specializes in old railway lanterns. It also has an exhibit announced as the only one of its kind in the world: a large glass case full of 19th-century stuffed frogs posed in the silliest endeavours—playing billiards or teaching class or eating spaghetti.

Lake of Bienne

Prehistory and modern industry meet in **Bienne,** called Biel in German (pop. 58,000), a prosperous, cheerful town of rivers, brooks, canals and the lake of the same name. The new shopping district is airy and tempting. The old town, with medieval houses cleverly restored to look as old as they are, lures the visitor to stroll, stop and stare. The 16th-century fountains catch the eye, their statues painted in outlandish colours.

Prehistory is a Bienne preoccupation because of the achievements of a local archaeologist, Frédéric Schwab (1803–96). The ancient tools, weapons and ornaments he

Blind but colourful, Justice stands above typical Neuchâtel fountain.

found at La Tène (near the shore of Lake Neuchâtel) gave the name in French to the second Iron Age: *l'époque de La Tène.* Bienne's museum was donated to the town by Schwab, after whom it is named. Many of its prehistoric and Roman relics were unearthed by the colonel himself.

Bienne enjoys—or suffers from—an intriguing linguistic situation. About two-thirds of the population speak Swiss-German, the rest French. Virtually everyone in Bienne is bilingual of necessity.

Excursion boats on the lake of Bienne go to **St. Peter's Island** *(L'Ile de Saint-Pierre/St. Petersinsel)*—about a 50-minute trip, one-way. This nature preserve is known as the largest island in Switzerland, a modest enough superlative, but no longer valid; because the water level has been lowered in an extensive drainage project, it is now a peninsula. The island captured the heart of that early ecologist, Jean-Jacques Rousseau, on a visit here in 1765. His hotel room, filled with memorabilia, is a place of pilgrimage nowadays. Otherwise the attractions haven't changed: flowered fields of grazing horses, a few vineyards and peaceful, quite penetrable forests.

Lake of Morat

Too small for a local bus service, the town of **Morat** does have a train station and ferryboats on its own little lake. Like Bienne, Morat is bilingual; the German-speaking majority call it Murten, and so do most maps.

This jewel of a town is a wonder of perfectly preserved old houses with deep arcades and overhanging roofs. You can climb up to the medieval towers and ramparts to survey the tile roofs, the lake and the countryside. Morat's defences also call to mind the battle of June 22, 1476, in which the Confederates relieved the besieged town and massacred the army of Charles the Bold.

It would take an accomplished bungler to get lost in Morat, but the tourist office has gone to the trouble of issuing a map which shows all three streets. With or without a map, you'll notice the 13th-century château, the solid Berne Gate *(Berntor)* with its clock and belfry, and the French- and German-speaking churches. Every building in the old town has a style and charm of its own, with only this in common: after a great fire in 1416 the municipal building code required all houses to be constructed of stone, with tile roofs.

Fribourg
Pop. 39,000

Many a beautiful city has been set alongside a river, but Fribourg is a special case. The tormented terrain makes it a three-dimensional town, built both alongside and overhanging its river, the Sarine (Saane in German). An unaccountable harmony binds the fine Gothic buildings with the brutally deep gorges and the pastoral scene beyond. In Fribourg even the simple joys—a covered bridge or a public fountain—become profound.

Fribourg was settled in 1157 by Duke Berchtold IV of Zähringen, who liked its defensive location. In 1481 Fribourg joined the Swiss Confederation. When the Protestant Reformation took over its sister city, Berne, Fribourg resisted. And it remains a visibly Catholic town of churches, seminaries, religious bookshops and a profusion of nuns and priests bustling about the streets.

It's also a bilingual sort of place. Since the 15th century, when Latin was abandoned as the bureaucratic language, French and German have alternated in power. French finally won in 1830—but is now losing ground.

To begin with the dramatic setting of Fribourg: the Zähringen Bridge offers the classic panorama with the river running beneath, the 13th- and 14th-century ramparts on the steep hillside and the old covered bridge linking the Sarine's banks. There has been a bridge at this point since the 13th century, though it has had to be replaced after every major flood. Then from the modern Gottéron Bridge above the river, you look back to the city with its red tile roofs and the 15th-century cathedral tower.

Like all the historic buildings of Fribourg, the **Cathédrale de St-Nicolas** is built of local sandstone. Age, weather and the vibration and pollution of the traffic are taking a visible toll, so a ten-year restoration programme is under way. Sad to say, the Gothic statues around the main portal are fakes; because of the atmospheric conditions the originals had to be moved indoors—to the Catholic University. Inside the cathedral, look for the Chapel of the Holy Sepulchre with its touching 15th-century sculptural ensemble, *The Entombment*. And notice two elements in very different styles: a florid 19th-century organ and 20th-century stained-glass windows.

Another important focus of artistic interest is the Franciscan church, **Eglise des Cordeliers.** Behind its rather routine 18th-century façade is an imposing church with some outstanding religious paintings and sculptures—*The Triptych* over the main altar (1480) and the carved wooden *Retable of Furno* (1513).

Just up the street, Fribourg's **Musée d'Art et d'Histoire** (art and history) occupies a Renaissance mansion called the Hôtel Ratzé. Almost everything on view—from an ornate 2,500-year-old dagger to romantic paintings—originated in Fribourg and vicinity. The town has always been richly supplied with religious art, particularly sculpture, and this is well displayed, starting with a fascinating 10th-century crucifixion scene in stone.

Fribourg's **town hall** (*Hôtel de Ville* or *Rathaus*) has a tall, steep roof, a covered ceremonial staircase and a Germanic clock tower. Across the square, with its typical Fribourg statue-fountain, is a venerable linden tree—according to tradition, more than 500 years old. When the Swiss defeated Charles the Bold at Morat, it is said, the commander of the Fribourg troops despatched a runner to spread the good news. Arriving at this very spot, the courier cried, "Victory!" with his last breath and died instantly from his heroic exertions. The story goes that the little branch of linden which decorated the messenger's hat was planted to commemorate the event. Fastidious historians now insist the tree is even older than the Battle of Morat, which rather spoils the tale. Every October thousands of runners retrace the path between Morat and Fribourg in Switzerland's most popular race.

Around Fribourg

Avenches. Age-old mysteries lurk in and under the drowsy hill town of Avenches, born as Aventicum. It became a city of perhaps 20,000 people, the capital of Roman Helvetia. In about A.D. 260 the dreaded Alamanni tribesmen breached the 25-foot encircling wall and sacked the town. No one knows what happened then, whether the inhabitants were wiped out or marched away or enslaved. But overnight Aventicum died. A new town was founded on the same hill in the Middle Ages but it never became more

Fribourg: dark-green river flows round the red-tiled medieval city.

than a shadow of the original prosperous capital. Today, too small to have a parking problem, Avenches is a crossroads of memories.

At the end of the main street (Rue Centrale) is the **Amphitheatre** which in Roman times seated about 8,000 spectators. You can see parts of the tunnel system through which the wild animals, gladiators or acrobats entered the ring. Just above the main entrance to the arena stands a medieval tower, now the **Roman Museum.** Everything is well presented here, and it all comes from Aventicum.

Payerne. The abbey church of Payerne, **L'Abbatiale,** has had an unusually chequered history, but once you've found your way inside you can't fail to be moved by its grandeur. It is, simply, Switzerland's greatest Romanesque church.

Originally, perhaps in the 4th century, a Roman villa occupied the site. In the 10th century

a church was built there by order of Payerne's most distinguished citizen, the Burgundian Queen Berthe, who was also the mother-in-law of Otto the Great, first of the Holy Roman emperors. In the 11th century a much larger church was established, with technical assistance from the Benedictine abbey of Cluny in eastern France. After the Reformation the great old church was abandoned; it served variously as a barn, barracks and prison. But more than 50 years of restoration work has revealed many of Payerne's medieval glories—most strikingly, the majestic columns soaring up to the barrel-vaulted roof. They are constructed of layers of stone, alternately light and darker. The absence of furniture or decorations enhances the single-

Taking the sun in Switzerland's quaintest village, Gruyères; flowers embellish Renaissance windows.

minded, reverent effect. You'll see partly restored frescoes but the most important works of art are kept in an upstairs chapel reached by a modern wooden staircase. Here are Romanesque stone sculptures of birds, animals, and saintly men with troubled faces.

The abbey is part of an architectural compound comprising a castle and two churches. If you find yourself admiring the modern stained-glass windows, wooden ceilings and the blue-, yellow- and white-patterned walls, then you are in the 14th-century parish church *(Eglise Paroissiale)*— new by Payerne standards.

Romont. The streets in this farmer's market town on a hill are unexpectedly wide, because a 15th-century fire erased the original, cramped layout. The fire had no effect on the 13th-century ramparts. They still encircle the fine château, the church and several streets of pleasant houses built after the conflagration. You can walk the walls, enjoying a view all the way to Mont-Blanc and listening to the soprano bells of the sheep, the contralto bells of the cows and the tenor of the church clock-tower.

The church *(La Collégiale)* is an impressive Gothic structure with admirable medieval and modern stained-glass windows.

Lucens. The medieval château of Lucens has been privately owned since 1801. The latest proprietor is a Zurich antique house, which has filled the very roomy castle with authentic old furniture and works of art. Everything you see on the 45-minute guided tour is for sale!

In a vaulted cellar of the castle is a Sherlock Holmes museum with a replica of the storied lodgings at 221 B Baker Street. Adrian Conan Doyle, son of the creator of Holmes and Watson, lived in the château for ten years.

Oron. The impregnable-looking Château d'Oron manages to have a lived-in air. You may even arrive during a candlelit banquet. The antiques and rare books are *not* for sale.

Gruyères. Along the cobbled main street of Gruyères, pipe-smoking farmers in clodhoppers sit on benches staring at tourists taking pictures of the delightful old houses. It is one of those too-good-to-be-true, storybook towns.

This fortified medieval town sitting cozily atop its own hill owes its name to the counts of Gruyères. In the Middle Ages they owned a hefty chunk of Switzerland. Their château was first built in the 12th century, then considerably expanded and improved in the 15th. However, by the mid-16th century feudalism was on the wane and the last of the counts went bankrupt. Creditors from Fribourg and Berne took over.

The **château** is worth visiting, if only for the view from the battlements over the soft green countryside and up to jagged mountains. The worn steps of the spiral staircase lead to well-preserved state and private rooms. In many parts of the castle and the town you'll see the symbol of the counts of Gruyères, a crane (*grue* in French). One story goes that a white bird very much like a crane miraculously appeared in the sky to mark the spot where a castle should be built.

Gruyères has come to terms with its situation as one of Switzerland's foremost tourist attractions. It is hospitable to the throngs of visitors and offers food and drink (try the delicious double cream over berries or in meringues) and all manner of souvenirs: cowbells, miniature alpine horns, ceramics and wooden cream-pots. But cars and tour buses are barred from the town.

At the edge of town is a modern cheese factory (open to the public) where the renowned Gruyère cheese is made.

What to Do

Sports

The Swiss fully appreciate the beauty of their country. They're also crazy about fresh air and physical fitness. So when it comes to sports, they're doers more than watchers. Hardly any outdoor sports are neglected here, from the most strenuous cross-country skiing to the most sedate lakeside angling. Take your pick.

Skiing

Late November to early April is the season in most resorts, but the conditions vary from year to year and mountain to mountain. The Christmas and Easter holiday periods are the high seasons for prices and crowds, when you have to get to the lifts early in the morning to avoid bottlenecks. To escape the peak prices look into package tours which include hotel, meals and ski instruction. For whole families, flats and chalets may be rented. A middle course is the so-called *hôtel garni* which provides the housing but no restaurant, permitting you to eat more adventurously.

If you're unaccustomed to high-altitude skiing you'll have

to take special care to avoid sunburn or snow-blindness. Always wear plenty of clothes, even in apparently balmy weather, since conditions can change rapidly in the mountains. The altitude itself can be debilitating. Statistics show that most skiers who are injured succumb either on the first or last day of their holidays—in the first case due to lack of preparation, and in the latter because, overconfident, they were eager for one final thrill.

Cross-country skiing has seen an enormous surge in popularity in recent years. New trails open up every season. The Swiss Ski Federation puts out a booklet with details. Some of the best spots for this vigorous and invigorating sport can be found in the Jura and in the Sarine Valley between Château d'Oex and Gstaad.

Other Winter Sports

Ski-bobs, a sort of down-to-earth low-profile form of skiing—a bobsled built for one. They can be rented at the resorts, some of which reserve special slopes for them.

Ice-skating. Most ski resorts have natural ice rinks; some have artificial rinks as well. Skates and lessons are available on the spot.

Curling. This sport, as inscrutable as ice-fishing, is practised in many resorts, either in the open or in more comfortable covered ice-rinks.

Summer sports

High-altitude resorts take advantage of the eternal snows to offer summer skiing. It's quite common for holiday-makers to ski in the morning and swim in the afternoon. Many resorts keep their aerial cableways and ski-lifts operating in summer for the benefit of hikers and mountain-climbers, as well as sedentary sightseers.

Mountain climbing. Expert guidance and proper equipment are vital. Rescue personnel sometimes find that accident victims are dressed for a tennis match instead of a challenging encounter with nature at its trickiest. The only sensible course for the inexperienced is to join a mountain-climbing school.

Hiking. Switzerland is amazingly well organized in this respect. Everywhere you wander you'll see yellow signs marking the footpaths and estimating how long it will take to reach your destination. Many books, leaflets and maps are available suggesting walks through the most attractive countryside.

Swimming. Visitors accustomed to the Gulf Stream may find the mountain lakes a bit chilly, but most towns have public pools with comfortable temperatures. Pools and beaches are equipped with changing facilities.

Boating. You can hire a pedalo or a yacht on Swiss lakes,

though you need a licence to captain a boat with more than 15 square metres of sail. Winds on the lakes can be exceedingly unpredictable because of the surrounding mountains.

Water-skiing. This expensive sport can be pursued on several lakes. At Estavayer-le-Lac on Lake Neuchâtel a water ski tow eliminates the need for a motorboat.

Fishing. Local police stations cheerfully issue fishing licences by the day, week or month.

Golf. Any place big enough to be called a plateau probably has a golf course. And what scenery! Normally members of golf clubs abroad can play Swiss courses for a greens fee.

Tennis. Most big resorts have courts, as do the principal towns—though municipal facilities are often crowded. Lessons can usually be arranged.

Riding. Stables, riding schools and "ranches" may be found near cities and in resort areas. Some places organize cross-country riding holidays.

Cycling. Switzerland thinks of everything! You can rent a bike at any railway station and turn it in at a station farther along the line whenever you get tired. But don't forget that there's a lot of uphill pedalling!

Festivals and Folklore

No Swiss village is so small that it doesn't stage a festival once, or more likely several times, a year. A convention of yodellers, a saint's day, the blooming of the tulips, the anniversary of a local battle, a wine harvest—or no reason at all—may touch off days and nights of festivity. Choirs sing, bands march, children dance, actors declaim, flags fly, and everyone eats and drinks a good deal. Often the whole town will be involved in months of rehearsal and preparation for a grandiose spectacle; a cast of thousands, including livestock, is not unheard of.

The Swiss National Tourist Office publishes a leaflet listing all the country's local events far in advance. Or you can simply ask your hotel receptionist if there are any *fêtes* scheduled in the area.

If it's yodelling you're after, you may have to go to the German-speaking part of Switzerland. But folk dancing and country songs, accompanied by puffing accordions, turn up everywhere. You may even hear the *cor des Alpes* (alpine horn), a bizarre instrument twice as long as a man is tall.

Swiss wrestling (*lutte suisse*) is a rare sport with roots far back in history. The gladiators, dressed in special short trousers, struggle fiercely while maintaining strict rules of chivalry.

Heading for a fall: wrestlers grapple in bout of age-old Swiss sport.

Nightlife

"Swinging Switzerland" is not quite the description. For one thing, work starts too early the next morning. But considering that Swiss cities are small towns by European standards, the after-dark situation is much livelier than might be expected.

Even in relatively isolated places you'll probably find what you're looking for—whether a disco or a country dance, a convivial café or a concert.

For the most frenzied nightlife you have to go to what one cynic has dubbed the snow supermarkets, the big ski resorts. Here all conditions conspire to heat up the recreation-by-moonlight—the altitude, fresh air, sense of physical well-being, absence of routine cares and a contagious *joie de vivre.* The music blares far into the night, and ski-strained muscles work overtime on the dance floor.

Geneva, the biggest and most international city in French-speaking Switzerland, is also the region's nightlife capital. Clubs with floor-shows, dance bands and even professional dancing partners flourish until 4 a.m.—not quite what Calvin had in mind for his citizens. The prime concession to propriety is the low-key advertising—inconspicuous photos of the chorus girls in their non-costumes and no neon lights.

Elsewhere, the entertainment may be less professional—a local folklore group or a strolling band of Spanish troubadours. But what more could

anyone want while nursing a carafe of wine alongside a roaring fire in a mountain lodge?

Or, on a fine summer night, you can board one of the Lake of Geneva steamers shanghaied for a dancing cruise. The romantic ingredients are convincing—the music, the lake, the stars and the Alps for inspiration.

If you seek more serious entertainment you won't be all at sea in Switzerland. Even the small towns hold concerts and recitals by first-rate artists. And what could be more effective than medieval music in the courtyard of a château or an organ recital in a historic church?

Geneva is the regional centre for opera. Both Geneva and Lausanne are keen on ballet. Famous orchestras make the rounds of Swiss concert halls—most often in Geneva and Lausanne but also in Fribourg, Neuchâtel and Montreux, among others. The Geneva-based Orchestre de la Suisse Romande performs all over the country as well as abroad. Fine local and guest choral groups can frequently be heard.

Jazz, traditional or far-out, is not neglected. All the regional concerts of the year are just a warm-up for the summer's summit meeting on the Vaud

Riviera, the internationally watched Jazz Festival of Montreux.

Both local theatre troupes and touring companies from France perform in the cities. Outdoor shows are often scheduled in the summer. Just about everything is in French.

Most cinemas show films dubbed into French, but in big towns and tourist areas they may be projected in *version originale* ("v.o." in the advertisements), meaning the original-language soundtrack plus subtitles in French and German.

Shopping

Of course you'll want to check on the cheese, chocolate, clocks and watches. But the frontiers of shopping in Switzerland are much more expansive. And, alas, expensive.

Because of the solidity of the Swiss franc, visitors from most countries find the price-tags here discouragingly high. Even so, you're sure of the best quality. The Swiss themselves may well be the world's most demanding customers.

When to Shop
Monday is the unpredictable day, depending on the town you're in or the kind of shop you want. To be on the safe side, assume the worst: that your shop is closed for the morning every Monday, as many are. On normal weekdays early-bird Swiss start shopping about 8 or 8.30 a.m. and keep at it until about 6.30 or 6.45 p.m. (Saturdays until 5 p.m.). Small shops normally close for lunch, as do many businesses.

What to Buy
Antiques. Towns and tourist resorts have inviting antique shops with very high-quality merchandise, some of it museum worthy. If you're looking for bargains–which are unlikely–browse around the antique stands in street markets.

Art. Galleries galore in towns like Geneva and Lausanne and even in small, out-of-the-way places. Experts point out that in this field the prices in Switzerland are no higher than anywhere else. The dealers are accustomed to shipping paintings and sculptures to the ends of the earth.

Brandies. Potent and portable, Swiss spirits make a long-lasting souvenir or gift. They're made from apples *(pomme)*, cherries *(kirsch)*, grapes *(marc)*, pears *(poire)*, plums *(pruneau)* or alpine herbs *(gentiane)*.

Cheese. Depending on where you live and how long it will take you to get there, you might be interested in carrying away a variety of Swiss cheeses. Some are very long-lasting. Ask in any cheese shop for advice on which varieties are practical as souvenirs.

Cigars. Relations between Switzerland and Cuba have never wavered. Here you'll find the very best Havana cigars kept in perfect condition—extremely expensive but, for *aficionados*, pure heaven.

Cuckoo-clocks. All sizes and styles are sold in department stores and souvenir shops but they usually come from Germany. If they're too silly for your taste, think about a sober Swiss alarm clock.

Dolls. Outfitted in regional costumes. People in isolated parts of the Valais still wear traditional garb in daily life but elsewhere only on very special occasions.

Jewellery. Plenty of gold, mostly the expensive white gold, in tasteful, simple forms. Stones of impeccable quality are also part of the tradition. Look over the glamorous displays in principal shopping streets, but don't forget the small artisan shops often hidden away in the neighbourhoods of the Old Town.

Embroidered handwork. Tablecloths, aprons, handkerchiefs and pincushions make wonderful gifts and can be found in different price ranges.

Knives. The Swiss army invention—essentially a pocket tool-kit—comes in many sizes and prices. The big ones contain a magnifying glass, corkscrew, nailfile and scissors.

Masks. To the casual eye they may resemble African masks but they're Swiss—from the mountain villages of the Valais. For people who can't bear the thought of taking home a plastic gnome.

Pottery. A traditional Swiss speciality. Look for pewter, too.

Shoes. Expensive by most standards but the quality is unarguably tops. Or if you arrived unequipped for a mountain hike...

Souvenirs. Alpenstocks, miniature cowbells, copper pots, glass figurines, music boxes.

Toys. Hand-made wooden toys are original and appealing.

Watches. It's a flattering fact that tourists from the countries whose watch industries give

Art and commerce united in show window of Geneva jewellery shop.

Switzerland the most painful competition always make a beeline for Swiss watch shops... not for bargains but for the quality. There are good shops everywhere, so it's just a matter of finding the style of watch that suits you best. Be sure it comes with an international guarantee.

Wining and Dining

The seasons and the scenery add to the pleasure of dining out in Switzerland.* In winter, you can thaw out in a rustic wood-panelled *carnotzet*, a cozy sort of place serving simple food. In spring, lakeside establishments set up shop outdoors on open terraces. Mountainside restaurants mix *haute cuisine*, high altitude and dazzling views. Or you can sample the atmosphere of country inns or big-city *brasseries* or super-luxury restaurants so expensive that even visiting oil sheiks read the menu from right to left.

Most restaurants in the region serve Swiss-French food, mostly a hearty, country style of cooking. Fine French cuisine can also be found, as well as *la nouvelle cuisine* where the sauces are lighter and the combinations of flavour offbeat. You may be surprised at the proliferation of Italian-style restaurants; pizzas are as popular here as *fondues*. Other nationalities are represented, mostly in the more cosmopolitan towns—Chinese, German, Greek, Indian, North African,

---

* For a comprehensive guide to French and German culinary terms, consult the Berlitz EUROPEAN MENU READER

Spanish and Vietnamese, for instance.

Wherever you go, the service is good and the portions gargantuan. Incidentally, many restaurants serve second helpings, on a clean plate, as big as the first. Just keep your knife and fork... and your determination to struggle on. Because the main course is usually a meal in itself, many Swiss have only a salad or consommé as a starter.

Most restaurants advertise one or more dishes of the day, from a set meal to a single filling dish (assiette du jour or plat du jour). Ordering the day's special may save you money and the service will be quicker.

Here's a very Swiss eccentricity: as you eat and drink, cash-register tickets are placed in a small wineglass or under a salt-shaker on your table. At the end of the meal the waiter or waitress will add them all up, tell you how much you owe and collect the money.

The service charge is included in the price in all cafés and restaurants in Switzerland. But you can always leave a few coins for exceptionally good service.

Swiss Specialities

Fondue is filling and fun to eat. The celebrants sit around a bubbling cauldron watching their chunks of bread, speared on special long forks, cooking in a mixture of cheeses diluted with white wine and a dash of kirsch.

Fondue bourguignonne. The scene is the same but the pot is filled with boiling oil, and the diners dip their pieces of steak in. After each bite is cooked, flavour it with one of the different sauces.

Fondue chinoise, the "Chinese" version. Impale a paper-thin slice of meat on a long fork and immerse it in a boiling pot of broth. The last act, after you've cooked and eaten all your meat, is to drink the delicious resultant soup.

Raclette. A less famous cousin of *fondue* featured in the mountains and in city restaurants with the necessary equipment. Half a big wheel of cheese is brought close to a heating element. As it begins to melt, the cook scrapes off a layer—crispy at best—onto your plate. Eaten with boiled potatoes (peel them before you eat them), pickled onions and gherkins. It's often served on an eat-as-much-as-you-can basis *(à discrétion).*

An important note about cheese *fondue* and *raclette:* you're not supposed to drink anything cold with or immedi- **93** ately after these dishes. Only white wine or hot tea are advised. Breaking this unwritten rule, even for a glass of water, can be risky for your digestive tract.

Two cheese specialities that make good snacks or light meals: *ramequins*, cheese tarts, and *croûte au fromage*, a sort of open-faced melted cheese sandwich.

Fish Dishes

Swiss lakes provide a good variant in the local diet. The fish may be grilled or sautéed in a wine sauce or just converted into fish-and-chips. Among the local delicacies:

Omble chevalier (char). Hard-to-catch king of the lake, which is frequently poached and served with hollandaise.

Truite (trout). The lake

Breadline, Swiss style: a bakery-restaurant lures with its loaves.

variety is often big enough to feed a family. *Truite saumonée* (salmon trout) is a tender cousin with slightly pink flesh.

Brochet (pike). Another big lake fish offered grilled or as *quenelles de brochet*—fluffy dumplings of ground fish bathed in a white-wine sauce.

Perche (perch). Usually served filleted and fried with a slice of lemon and tartar sauce or *meunière*, sautéed in butter.

Féra (dace). Savoury fish that turns up baked or sautéed.

Meat Dishes

Assiette Valaisanne. A simple and pleasing cold plate from the Valais—*viande séchée* (very thin slices of dried beef), cured ham, dried bacon and sausages, local cheese and gherkins. Eaten with *pain de seigle*, rich dark-rye bread, and almost inevitably with Fendant wine.

Game *(chasse):* In season, many restaurants feature hare, venison and game birds, often in heavy red-wine sauce.

Sausages: French and German influences meet in these back-country specialities. Try the *saucisse de veau*, a white, mild-flavoured veal sausage, or the *saucisson vaudois*, a spicy smoked sausage served with green beans or in a *papet* with leeks and potatoes. *Paire de Vienne* (hotdogs) and *Schüblig* (a longer, stronger version) appear everywhere with potato salad or, if you're lucky, with *rösti*, the great German-Swiss "discovery" a few degrees more sophisticated than American hash-browned potatoes. Boiled, cut up and fried with bacon bits to a golden brown, *rösti* are not exactly fluffy or trivial but justly renowned.

Emincé zurichoise. A Zurich speciality found all over Switzerland—slivers of veal and mushrooms in a cream sauce. Another excuse to order *rösti*. **95**

Cheese

You came to the right country. But, strangely enough, few restaurants serve cheese platters in the French style. This may prompt you to visit a cheese shop or the market and pick up the makings of a picnic.

Emmental is the mild, holey cheese known in some other countries as Swiss cheese.

Gruyère looks similar, but no holes, and is nuttier and harder; sold in different degrees of saltiness.

Vacherin Mont-d'Or is an unctuous, runny treat that comes in a round wooden box. Available only in winter.

Tête de Moine is a hard, round pungent cheese that does look rather like the head of a bald monk.

Tomme vaudoise, a flat, mild, soft cheese, sometimes with caraway seeds.

Reblochon, a soft, creamy, delicious white cheese but often a bit smelly.

Desserts

If the momentum has propelled you this far you might try a *tarte* or *gâteau*, perhaps an apple or plum pie or *tarte au vin* (made with either red or white wine), or a *coupe Danemark* (ice-cream sundae with chocolate sauce and mountains of whipped cream). In season, savour some fresh *fraises* (strawberries), *framboises* (raspberries) or *mûres* (blackberries) with heavy cream. *Vermicelle*, squiggles of puréed chestnut smothered with whipped cream, is very popular.

Or you may prefer to wait an hour or two, have a bit of exercise and then drop into any bakery where the choice of enticing pastry will provide the day's most difficult decision.

Coffee

The Swiss drink small cups of coffee, often adding cream, but for breakfast it's usually *café au lait*, coffee mixed with hot milk. It is weaker than French or Italian coffee. If you crave an espresso, ask for *un ristretto*—in Italian!

Swiss Wines

When people in western Switzerland discuss wine, they're talking about the product of the next hillside, or the village just around the bend. They take their wines seriously—and copiously. If you're interested in wines, this is a good place to pursue your studies. It's also a

In typical Valaisan cave, a choice of classic cheeses and local wines.

refreshing way to meet the locals.

You can sample Swiss wines haphazardly, which is amusing enough, or somewhat more methodically by taking advantage of the facilities organized by the wine trade:

Caves, the vast wine-cellars where the product is aged and bottled. Some companies run guided tours, followed by tasting sessions and (they hope) the purchase of a bottle or two.

Caveaux, small wine-cellars run by the men who grow the grapes; you sample the local vintages and meet the people responsible for them. Of course, the vintners are also interested in selling their wine.

Pintes, friendly bars in which local wines and hearty food go well together.

Local tourist offices have leaflets and lists of addresses, as well as detailed maps of wine-growing regions for seeing and tasting.

How to Drink

In a bar or restaurant wine is ordered by the bottle or half-bottle, or by the carafe in multiples of one decilitre (one-tenth of a litre). A normal bottle of wine contains seven decilitres, so if you order, for example, a carafe of *cinq décis*
98 (five decilitres, half a litre), it's

the equivalent of five-sevenths of a bottle.

In many establishments it simply won't do to order "*rouge*" or "*blanc*" without specifying the region. If the wine list (often spoken, not written, in bars) leaves you confused, ask the waiter for advice.

As a general rule, white wine is drunk with fish, white meat and hot cheese dishes such as fondue; red wine with red meat and game; and rosé goes well with fish. The Swiss also sip little glasses of white wine as an aperitif.

The Regions

The Valais is the biggest wine-producing canton in Switzerland. You'll see Europe's loftiest vineyards here, some as high as 3,600 feet above sea level. The best known wines of the Valais are white: the fruity Fendant and the slightly more alcoholic Johannisberg made from Sylvaner grapes. As for reds, try the pleasant Goron or the full-flavoured, ruby-coloured Dôle or Pinot Noir.

White wine from the canton of Vaud is classified as Dorin; they can be light and lively or somewhat flinty. The best red wines, Salvagnin and Pinot Noir, are mellow and fragrant.

In the canton of Geneva, the white Perlan wines are mild

and fruity; the reds are labelled Gamay.

Neuchâtel is a considerably smaller producer but there are dry sprightly whites, some full-bodied reds, a rosé, and even a presentable bubbly wine resembling champagne.

Other Drinks

Swiss lager beers are sold under various brand-names in bottles and on tap. The best-known imported labels, principally German and Alsatian are also widely available. For non-alcoholic drinks, try the excellent local juices, particularly grape and apple juice. Mineral water, still or bubbly, Swiss or imported, may be found everywhere.

After-dinner Drinks

Swiss fruit brandies are popular with after-dinner drinkers. These colourless potions are usually served in alarmingly big, stemmed glasses, and they pack a punch. *Pomme* is apple brandy, *pruneau* is made of plums and *kirsch* is cherry brandy. *Poire William*, a pear brandy, sometimes comes in a bottle with an actual pear enclosed. *Marc* is a very strong eau-de-vie derived from the residue of the wine-pressing. Not for the faint-hearted.

Santé!

To Help You Order...

Could we have a table?
Do you have a set menu?

Pouvons-nous avoir une table?
Avez-vous un menu du jour?

I'd like a/an/some...

J'aimerais...

beer	**une bière**	menu	**la carte**
butter	**du beurre**	milk	**du lait**
bread	**du pain**	mineral water	**de l'eau minérale**
cheese	**du fromage**	plate	**une assiette**
coffee	**un café**	potatoes	**des pommes de**
cream	**de la crème**		**terre**
(whipped)	**(fouettée)**	salad	**une salade**
dessert	**un dessert**	sandwich	**un sandwich**
fish	**du poisson**	soup	**de la soupe**
glass	**un verre**	sugar	**du sucre**
ice-cream	**une glace**	tea	**du thé**
lemon	**du citron**	water	**de l'eau**
meat	**de la viande**	wine	**du vin**

...and Read the Menu

agneau	lamb	haricots verts	green beans
ail	garlic	jambon	ham
artichaut	artichoke	langue	tongue
asperges	asparagus	lapin	rabbit
aubergine	eggplant	lard	bacon
bœuf	beef	lièvre	hare
canard, caneton	duck, duckling	macédoine de fruits	fruit salad
céleri	celery (root)	médaillon	tenderloin
champignons	mushrooms	morilles	morel mushrooms
chantilly	whipped cream	moules	mussels
chevreuil	venison	moutarde	mustard
chou	cabbage	navets	turnips
chou-fleur	cauliflower	nouilles	noodles
concombre	cucumber	œufs	eggs
côte(lette)	chop, cutlet	oignons	onions
courgettes	baby marrow (zucchini)	oseille	sorrel
		petits pois	green peas
cuisses de grenouilles	frogs' legs	poire	pear
		poireaux	leeks
dinde	turkey	pomme	apple
écrevisse	crayfish	porc	pork
endives	chicory (endives)	potage	soup
		poulet	chicken
entrecôte	steak	prune, pruneau	plum
épinards	spinach		
escalope	veal cutlet	raisins	grapes
escargots	snails	riz	rice
fenouil	fennel	rognons	kidneys
flageolets	beans	saucisse/ saucisson	sausage
foie	liver		
fraises	strawberries	saumon (fumé)	salmon (smoked)
frites	chips (French fries)	sorbet	water-ice (sherbet)
		terrine	pâté
framboises	raspberries	truite	trout
fruits de mer	seafood	vacherin cassis	black-currant frozen dessert
gigot (d'agneau)	leg of lamb		
gratin dauphinois	scalloped potatoes	veau	veal
		volaille	poultry

How to Get There

From North America

BY AIR: Non-stop flights leave most days of the week from New York to Geneva's Cointrin airport. Connecting flights are available from all major U.S. cities and more than a dozen Canadian cities. Alternatively you can fly to Zurich or Basel; there are daily, direct flights to Zurich from several North American cities.

APEX (Advance Purchase Excursion) fares must be purchased 30 days prior to departure. Tickets are good for stays of 14–90 days. These fares are lower from mid-October to mid-June and for mid-week travel. Round-trip youth fares for those between 12 and 21 are valid for one year and are cheaper during the same low season as the APEX fare.

Charter Flights and Package Tours. Winter packages feature ski tours, and other package arrangements offer stays of 7 to 14 days (or longer) with a choice of hotels and options for renting a car or purchasing a Eurailpass. Advance Booking Charters (ABC) must be booked 60 days before departure and include only the flight. The One-stop Inclusive Tour Charter (OTC) offers accommodation, transport and excursions.

Note: Visitors from outside Europe may travel on the Eurailpass, a flat-rate unlimited mileage ticket, valid for first-class rail travel anywhere in Western Europe outside Great Britain. Eurail Youthpass is similar to the Eurailpass, but offers second-class travel at a cheaper rate to anyone under 26.

From Great Britain and Eire

BY AIR: Regular scheduled flights leave for Zurich, Basel and Geneva daily from London. The most common types of fare besides first-class and economy are excursion tickets for stays of six days to one month, a special weekend (three-day) fare and the PEX and APEX fares. Certain airlines arrange fly/drive or fly/rail possibilities.

Package tours. There are frequent departures for Geneva and Zurich with many combinations of facilities from youth hostel or bed and breakfast in a simple establishment to full board in a five star hotel, all skiing arrangements included. You can even take advantage of the low cost of a package deal and make your own reservations for accommodation. Cancellation conditions are often stringent for package tours, so check in advance.

BY RAIL: The journey takes about 18 hours from London, so couchettes or sleepers should be reserved in advance. Ask at the Swiss National Tourist Office for special Holiday Tickets and Cards before leaving home; the Holiday Card gives you unlimited travel on trains, boats and coaches in Switzerland as well as free or cheaper travel on certain other services. The Holiday Ticket offers lower prices on certain routes. There are also reductions for senior citizens and young people, as well as other special fares such as family tickets.

BY ROAD: Book your passage well in advance for car ferries; midweek sailings are cheapest. Roads through France are good; the shortest route is via Calais or Boulogne to Paris, then from Paris to Geneva by motorway, which takes about 5 hours.

A regular coach service between London (Victoria) and Geneva operates several times weekly.

When to Go

Switzerland's modest area includes several mini-climates. When it's chilly and foggy in Geneva it may be sunny and warm in Sion and snowing in Champéry. Clear sunny days are frequent whether you come in spring, summer, autumn or winter.

Average monthly temperature (Geneva):

	J	F	M	A	M	J	J	A	S	O	N	D
°C	0	1	5	9	13	17	18	18	14	9	5	1.5
°F	33	34	41	48	55	63	64	64	57	48	41	34

Planning Your Budget

To give you an idea of what to expect, here are some average prices in Swiss francs. However, take into account that despite Switzerland's low inflation rate, all prices must be regarded as approximate.

Airport transfers. Airport bus to Geneva railway station Fr. 4, taxi about Fr. 25. Coach service from Geneva airport to Lausanne Fr. 18. Train from Zurich airport to railway station 2nd class Fr. 3.60

Bicycle hire. 4 hours Fr. 6, 12 hours Fr. 9, 24 hours Fr. 12.

Buses. Fr. 0.60 or 0.70 for up to 3 stops, Fr. 1 or 1.20 for 4 stops or more. 1-day ticket Fr. 3.50, 1-day Multi-City card Fr. 5, 3-day tourist pass Fr. 8.

Car hire. *Renault 5 TL* Fr. 35 per day, Fr. 0.47 per kilometre, Fr. 490 per week with unlimited mileage. *Ford Escort* Fr. 58 per day, Fr. 0.65 per km., Fr. 750 per week with unlimited mileage. *BMW 315/316* Fr. 105 per day, Fr. 1.09 per km., Fr. 1,288 per week with unlimited mileage.

Cigarettes. Fr. 1.90–3.10 for a packet of 20.

Hairdressers. *Man's* haircut Fr. 20–30. *Woman's* cut Fr. 23–30, shampoo and set Fr. 20–25, shampoo and blow-dry Fr. 25–30, permanent wave Fr. 60–70.

Hotels (double room with bath/shower per night). ***** Fr. 140–300, **** Fr. 90–190, *** Fr. 60–180, ** Fr. 50–110, * Fr. 50–90.

Meals and drinks. Continental breakfast Fr. 6–8, lunch/dinner in fairly good establishment Fr. 15–30, *fondue* from Fr. 12, coffee Fr. 1.70, glass of beer Fr. 1.70, ½ litre of table wine Fr. 8–10, soft drinks Fr. 2.50.

Shopping bag. Bread (500 grams) Fr. 1.50–2.50, butter (250 grams) Fr. 3–3.50, milk (litre) Fr. 1.45, 6 eggs Fr. 2–3.20, beefsteak (500 grams) Fr. 17–25, coffee (250 grams) Fr. 3.50–6, apple/orange juice (litre) Fr. 1.20–2.50, wine Fr. 3–15.

Ski-equipment hire. Cross-country from Fr. 15 a day, Fr. 70 a week. Downhill from Fr. 30 a day, Fr. 125–150 a week.

Swiss Holiday Card (2nd class). Fr. 125 for 4 days, Fr. 150 for 8 days, Fr. 190 for 15 days, Fr. 265 for a month (see also p. 121).

Taxi. Meter charge Fr. 4, plus Fr. 1.30 minimum per kilometre.

Trains (2nd class, one way). Geneva–Lausanne Fr. 12.80, Geneva–Zurich Fr. 46.

BLUEPRINT for a Perfect Trip

An A-Z Summary of Practical Information and Facts

Listed after most main entries is an appropriate translation, usually in the singular. You'll find this vocabulary useful when asking for assistance.
    For all prices, refer to list on page 103.

A   **ACCOMMODATION**—see **HOTELS, YOUTH HOSTELS**

AIRPORTS *(aéroport/Flughafen)*. Switzerland is served by three intercontinental airports: Geneva-Cointrin, Zurich-Kloten and Basel/Mulhouse. The Swiss national airline provides frequent flights connecting these three airports, and there are rail connections several times a day.

Passengers must generally check in 45 minutes before flight time—consult your airline to be sure. All three airports have snack bars and restaurants, news-stands, car-hire desks, banks, post offices and duty-free shops as well as boutiques offering a wide range of merchandise.

Self-service luggage carts can be found in the baggage claim area.

Ground transport (for rates, see page 103). In Geneva, a regular airport bus and city bus No. 33 run between Cointrin and the central railway station, Gare de Cornavin, a 15-minute ride away.

An airport coach service also links Geneva's airport with Lausanne (about every hour and a half); the trip takes 50 minutes.

Frequent train services connect Kloten airport with Zurich main railway station, Hauptbahnhof, 10 minutes away. It is also possible to reach Zurich-Kloten from many towns in French-speaking Switzerland by direct trains running at regular intervals.

In Basle, there's a frequent airport bus service to the air terminal at the central railway station.

Fly-baggage. By this system, you can register your luggage at many railway stations and next see it at the airport of your destination. You have to produce your airline ticket, and you may be required to check in your luggage up to 24 hours in advance, so ask at the local station first.

Private flights can land at Geneva airport as well as any one of Switzerland's 45 other airfields ranging from grass strips to elaborate installations. You can take a trip in light aircraft for a bird's-eye view of the Alps or for **air taxi** service within Switzerland. Check with the airport information desk.

Where's the bus for…?	**D'où part le bus pour…?**
What time does the bus leave for…?	**A quelle heure part le bus pour…?**

BABYSITTERS *(babysitter)*. Although private agencies exist which can be contacted by telephone, babysitters can be hired for half the price by getting in touch with one of the following: Bureau de Placement de l'Université in Geneva, tel. (022) 20 93 33, ext. 2701, or Croix Rouge de Lausanne (Red Cross, Lausanne section), (021) 23 66 16. Ask for *service babysitting*.

Remember to reserve a sitter a day ahead during the week; for the weekend you must call by 11 a.m. Friday.

Many resorts have *garderies* which take care of your children while you ski. The local tourist office should have the details.

BANKS and CURRENCY-EXCHANGE *(banque; change)*. Most banks are open from 8.30 a.m. to 12.30 p.m. and then from 1.30 to 4.30 or 5.30 p.m. Mondays through Thursdays, and from 8.30 to 5.30 or 6 p.m. non-stop on Fridays. Some banks in busy locations remain open during the lunch period every day and some do business on Saturday.

At airports and the larger railway stations, currency-exchange offices operate from 6.30 a.m. to 8 or 9 p.m., and sometimes even later, every day of the week. Ticket agents at railway stations will change foreign currency up to the price of your fare if the exchange office is closed.

Traveller's cheques are generally accepted everywhere, but banks will give you a better exchange rate than shops, hotels and restaurants. You must show your passport when you cash traveller's cheques.

See also CREDIT CARDS.

I want to change some pounds/dollars.	**Je voudrais changer des livres sterling/des dollars.**
Do you accept traveller's cheques?	**Acceptez-vous les chèques de voyage?**

BARBERS'—see **HAIRDRESSERS'**

B **BICYCLE HIRE** *(location de vélo)*. Nothing could be simpler: Rent a bicycle at a railway station and return it at any other station in Switzerland at no extra charge. Inquire at the luggage office of any main station. At smaller stations it's advisable to book the bike a day ahead. For rates see page 103.

Marked bicycle routes ranging from 10 to 60 kilometres are described in a booklet put out by the Union Cycliste Suisse, Rue du Vieux-Collège 4, 1204 Genève, tel. (022) 215206, or ask at the Touring Club Suisse, *section cyclistes,* listed in the phone book.

I'd like a map of bicycle routes near...	**J'aimerais une carte des itinéraires pour cyclistes de la région de...**

BOAT EXCURSIONS. One of the most popular summer activities is a lake cruise. On the Lake of Neuchâtel, you can go by boat from Neuchâtel to Morat (Lake of Morat) and Bienne (on the Lake of Bienne), passing by river from one lake to the other. Or just take a *tour* without getting off and dine on board.

The Lake of Geneva offers countless possibilities including trips to Evian and Thonon in France (35 minutes to Evian from Lausanne, another half-hour on to Thonon) where you can stop over and enjoy some French cuisine. The boats dock at almost all Swiss and French lakeside points and, if you prefer, you can come back by train. Tickets can be bought before or after boarding on most boat trips. Remember that the Eurailpass is also valid for these excursions.

The local tourist office can give you information about schedules, itineraries and buying tickets. For the Lake of Geneva, get in touch with the Compagnie Générale de Navigation sur le Lac Léman, Avenue de Rhodanie 17, 1000 Lausanne 6, tel. (021) 263535, or in Geneva at the Jardin-Anglais, tel. (022) 212521.

BUSES and TROLLEYBUSES *(bus; trolleybus)*. Swiss cities have efficient public transport services, which run frequently and are reasonably priced. For rates see page 103.

You buy a ticket from a vending machine, located at nearly every stop, before boarding. Although you don't show it to the driver an inspector may turn up en route to make a spot check. In most towns you can change buses on the same ticket; in Lausanne, you can transfer to the Métro. Routes are indicated on the vending machine. For tourists the best bargain may be a one-day ticket—*abonnement d'un jour*—or a three-day tourist pass (obtainable at principal bus stops or the main railway station) for unlimited travel on a town's public transport network.

Another possibility for those who want to visit several cities is the Multi-City card valid for the day for which it is stamped on public transport networks in more than 20 towns. It can be bought at the main ticket offices of each city's public transport system (the bus ticket office in the shopping mall below Cornavin station in Geneva or at Place St-François in Lausanne) and are good in Geneva, Lausanne, Neuchâtel, Fribourg, Bienne, Berne and Zurich to name a few. Ask for a *carte journalière multi-ville*.

Where's the nearest bus stop?	**Où se trouve l'arrêt de bus le plus proche?**

CAMPING. More than 275 campsites are approved by the Swiss Camping and Caravan Association, some at a height of more than 3,000 feet in the Alps. Many are open year-round with complete facilities. For a complete list of sites, rates and facilities, write the Fédération Suisse de Camping et de Caravanning, Habsburgerstrasse 35, Lucerne (or Post Box 24, 6003 Lucerne), tel. (041) 23 48 22, or get in touch with the local section of the Touring Club Suisse, Service Camping-Caravanning, listed in the phone directory. Remember that camping on private property or outside a recognized campsite requires permission.

Is there a camping site near here?	**Y a-t-il un camping dans les environs?**
May we camp here, please?	**Est-ce qu'on peut camper ici, s'il vous plaît?**
We have a tent/caravan (trailer).	**Nous avons une tente/caravane.**

CAR HIRE *(location de voitures).* Our PLANNING YOUR BUDGET section on page 103 lists the standard rates of the major car-hire firms, all of which operate throughout Switzerland.

To rent a car you must produce a valid driving licence which you've held for at least one year. You must be at least 18 years old (most firms require more). Agencies usually waive deposits for holders of authorized credit cards. If you want to turn in the car outside Switzerland you'll have to pay an extra charge. See also DRIVING.

I'd like to hire a car (for tomorrow).	**Je voudrais louer une voiture (pour demain).**
for one day/a week	**pour une journée/une semaine**
Please include full insurance.	**Avec casco complète, s'il vous plaît.**

CHEMISTS'—see **EMERGENCIES**

B

C

107

C   **CIGARETTES, CIGARS, TOBACCO** *(cigarette, cigare, tabac)*. Several well-known European and American brands of cigarettes are manufactured under licence in Switzerland, and local makes are also plentiful.

Pipe and cigar smokers will find every kind of pipe tobacco and cigars from the world over, including the best Cuban brands.

On the other hand, there are certain restrictions about smoking in public places. Smoking is banned in cinemas and on many buses. Public transport systems usually set aside areas for smokers (such as the sections in Swiss trains where red seats indicate *fumeurs*). For prices see page 103.

CLOTHING. Temperatures can vary within a few miles, a few hundred feet of altitude, or a few hours of the day—so it's best to be prepared for almost anything. In summer bring a raincoat or umbrella and a warm jacket or sweater as the weather can be changeable. In winter it's clear that appropriate clothing includes weatherproof coat and fur-lined boots if possible. For ski areas you should have sunglasses to protect your eyes from the glare. Don't plan to buy what you'll need after you arrive—clothing prices are among the highest in the world.

The Swiss dress rather conservatively with subdued colours and modest styles. If you go to a smart restaurant you may feel ill at ease without jacket and tie, but generally speaking informal and relaxed clothing is appropriate.

COMPLAINTS *(réclamation)*. Switzerland's tourist industry—particularly the hotel sector—prides itself on its service and takes complaints seriously. A word to the hotel manager should sort out any problem; if not, contact the tourist office. The same approach should settle any dissatisfaction in restaurants. Department stores have a customers' counter *(service clientèle)*; for the public transport system you should take your complaint to the main office.

CONSULATES and EMBASSIES *(consulat; ambassade)*. All embassies in the Swiss capital, Berne, have consular sections (for passport renewal, etc.) and some countries maintain consulates in Geneva:

Australia – Consulate: Rue de Moillebeau 56–58, 1209 Geneva; tel. (022) 346200. Hours: 9 a.m. to noon, 2–5 p.m., Mondays to Fridays. Embassy: Alpenstrasse 29, 3006 Berne; tel. (031) 430143. Hours: 8.30 a.m. to 12.30 p.m., 1.40–5 p.m., Mondays to Fridays (closed on **108** Friday afternoons).

Canada – Consulate: Avenue de Budé 8, 1202 Geneva; tel. (022) 33 90 00. Hours: 9–11.30 a.m., 2–4.30 p.m., Mondays to Fridays.

Embassy: Kirchenfeldstrasse 88, 3005 Berne; tel. (031) 44 63 81. Hours: 8 a.m. to noon, 1.30–5 p.m., Mondays to Fridays.

Eire – Embassy: Eigerstr. 71, 3007 Berne; tel. (031) 46 23 53. Hours: 10 a.m. to noon, 3–4 p.m., Mondays to Fridays.

South Africa – Embassy: Jungfraustrasse 1, 3005 Berne; tel. (031) 44 20 11. Hours: 9 a.m.–noon, 2–5 p.m., Mondays to Fridays.

United Kingdom – Consulate: Rue de Vermont 37–39, 1202 Geneva; tel. (022) 34 38 00. Hours: 8.30 a.m.–12.30 p.m., 2.30–4 p.m., Mondays to Fridays.

Embassy: Thunstrasse 50, 3005 Berne; tel. (031) 44 50 21. Hours: 9.30 a.m. to noon, 2.30–4 p.m., Mondays to Fridays.

United States of America – Consulate: Route de Pregny 11, 1292 Chambésy/Geneva; tel. (022) 99 02 11. Hours: 9 a.m. to noon, 2–4 p.m., Mondays to Fridays.

Embassy: Jubiläumsstrasse 93–95, 3005 Berne; tel. (031) 43 70 11. Hours: 9 a.m.–noon, 2–4 p.m., Mondays to Fridays.

CONVERTER CHARTS. For fluid and distance measures, see page 111. Switzerland uses the metric system.

Temperature

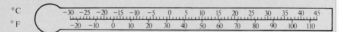

Length

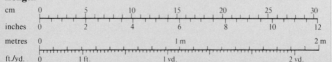

Weight

grams	0	100	200	300	400	500	600	700	800	900	1 kg
ounces	0	4	8	12	1 lb	20	24	28	2 lb.		

C **CREDIT CARDS** *(carte de crédit)*. Smaller businesses don't like to deal with credit cards, but they're widely used in major establishments. You'll find the signs prominently displayed at the entrance. See also CAR HIRE.

Do you accept credit cards? **Acceptez-vous les cartes de crédit?**

CURRENCY. The monetary unit of Switzerland is the Swiss franc (abbreviated Fr.), divided into 100 centimes (abbreviated c.). Coins include 5-, 10-, 20- and 50-centime pieces, as well as 1-, 2- and 5-franc pieces. Banknotes come in denominations of 10, 20, 50, 100, 500 and 1,000 francs.

CURRENCY EXCHANGE—see **BANKS**

CUSTOMS CONTROLS *(douane)*. The following chart shows what main duty-free items you may take into Switzerland and, when returning home, into your own country. For more detailed information it's wise to ask for the brochure provided by your customs service before you leave home.

Into:	Cigarettes		Cigars		Tobacco	Spirits		Wine
Switzer-land*	200 (400)	or	50 (100)	or	250 g. (500 g.)	1 l.	and	2 l.
Australia	200	or	250 g.	or	250 g.	1 l.	or	1 l.
Canada	200	and	50	and	900 g.	1.1 l.	or	1.1 l.
Eire	200	or	50	or	250 g.	1 l.	and	2 l.
N. Zealand	200	or	50	or	½ lb.	1 qt.	and	1 qt.
S. Africa	400	and	50	and	250 g.	1 l.	and	1 l.
U.K.	200	or	50	or	250 g.	1 l.	and	2 l.
U.S.A.	200	and	100	and	**	1 l.	or	1 l.

* The figures in parentheses are for non-European visitors only.
** A reasonable quantity.

Currency restrictions: You may import and export an unlimited amount of Swiss francs. See also ENTRY FORMALITIES.

I've nothing to declare.   **Je n'ai rien à déclarer.**
It's for my personal use.   **C'est pour mon usage personnel.**

DRIVING IN SWITZERLAND

Entering Switzerland: To bring your car into Switzerland you'll need:

- Your national driving licence
- Car registration papers
- Green Card (a recommended, but not obligatory extension to your regular insurance policy, making it valid for foreign countries)

You must have a nationality code sticker visible at the rear of the car, possess a red-reflector warning triangle for use in case you have a breakdown, and if you wear glasses, keep an extra pair in the glove compartment. Wearing your seat-belt is obligatory.

In winter, you may be required to use snow chains in the Alpine passes. These can be obtained at filling stations on the way.

Driving conditions: In Switzerland, you drive on the right and give priority to the right unless otherwise indicated. Especially when driving on mountain roads, don't allow yourself to be diverted by the awe-inspiring views; stop at roadside parking areas to admire peaks and gorges. On difficult stretches of mountain roads, priority is given to the ascending vehicle. The use of the horn is to be avoided everywhere, except on mountain roads with blind corners where on the contrary it's recommended.

Fluid measures

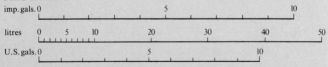

Distance

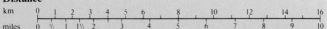

Speed limits: On the green signposted *autoroutes* (motorways/expressways) the maximum speed is 130 kph (kilometres per hour) which is **111**

D about 80 mph. On other roads the limit is 100 kph (about 60 mph) unless otherwise indicated. In residential areas speed is restricted to 50 kph (about 30 mph) and cars towing caravans may not exceed 80 kph (50 mph) even on motorways.

Breakdowns *(panne):* If you have a breakdown and belong to an automobile association in your country and have an AIT (Alliance Internationale de Tourisme) certificate, you'll get service free of charge from Touring Club Suisse (TCS). Of course you'll have to pay for spare parts. If you don't belong to a motoring organization you'll be charged the full bill for the patrolman or serviceman's help. On the motorways there are emergency telephones at regular intervals, about every mile. If you have a breakdown, press the button and help will come. Otherwise go to the nearest telephone and dial 140 for help.

Parking: More and more cities are establishing zones for pedestrians, especially in the central shopping and "old town" districts. Most big towns have parking meters and zones where parking is limited to 1½ hours *(zone bleue).* In other zones marked in red *(zone rouge)* you can park for 15 hours. You must place the dual clock-faced dial cards, given away at filling stations and banks, on the dashboard indicating when you left your car. Ask for a *disque de stationnement.*

Road signs: Most road signs used in Switzerland are the standard international pictographs. But here are a few other signs you might come across:

French	German	English
Aéroport	Flughafen	Airport
Centre-ville	Stadtzentrum	City centre
Déviation	Umleitung	Diversion (detour)
Douane	Zoll	Customs
Entrée	Auffahrt	Entrance
Fermé au trafic	Gesperrt	Closed to traffic
Hôpital	Spital	Hospital
Piétons	Fußgänger	Pedestrians
Sortie	Ausfahrt	Exit
Verglas	Glatteisgefahr	Icy road

driving licence	**permis de conduire**
car registration papers	**permis de circulation**
Are we on the right road for …?	**Sommes-nous sur la route de …?**

Fill the tank, please.	**Le plein, s'il vous plaît.**
normal/super	**normale/super**
Check the oil/tires/battery.	**Veuillez contrôler l'huile/les pneus/ la batterie.**
I've had a breakdown.	**Ma voiture est en panne.**
There's been an accident.	**Il y a eu un accident.**

DRY CLEANING—see **LAUNDRY**

ELECTRICITY. Standard voltage throughout Switzerland is 220-volt 50-cycle A.C. A small transformer may be required for your hair-dryer, but many electric razors have a switch which can be used for changing from one voltage to another.

EMBASSIES—see **CONSULATES**

EMERGENCIES *(urgence).* The following numbers should be useful in case of emergency in the French-speaking cantons:

Police 117	Emergency breakdown
Fire 118	advice 140

The information service, 111, can help you find other emergency numbers, such as ambulances. For less serious medical problems, many cities have a *permanence médicale* where you can get first-aid treatment 24-hours a day, or ask the operator for the number of the nearest hospital. Most large towns have a *permanence dentaire* for dental emergencies, which are open until 10 p.m. All phone numbers for emergency services are published daily in the local newspapers.

You can also find the name and address of the pharmacy *(pharmacie)* which is on 24-hour duty by consulting the day's local paper; or you can find the address posted in any pharmacy window after hours (one or more are on duty until 9 or 11 p.m. in large towns). See also MEDICAL CARE.

ENTRY FORMALITIES. See also CUSTOMS CONTROLS and DRIVING. Most visitors—including citizens of Britain, the U.S.A. and most other English-speaking countries—need only a valid passport to enter Switzerland. British subjects can use the simplified Visitor's Passport. Without further formality you are generally entitled to stay in Switzerland for up to 90 days.

113

G **GUIDES.** Many of the important sites and museums have brochures or part of the exhibits labelled in English. Some of Geneva's principal museums, as well as the botanical gardens, figure in a general brochure giving opening hours and how to get there. This pamphlet can be obtained in the museums or at the tourist office. Other museums, such as the Musée d'Art Brut in Lausanne, sell detailed guidebooks in English.

For individual guides, or for guided group tours of the region you should ask at the tourist office.

We'd like an English-speaking guide.	**Nous aimerions un guide parlant anglais.**
Do you have guided tours in English?	**Avez-vous des tours organisés en anglais?**
Do you have a brochure in English?	**Avez-vous une brochure en anglais?**

H **HAIRDRESSERS'** *(coiffeur)*. In major towns and resorts first-class hair stylists can always be found. Prices are high depending on the establishment, but a classic shampoo and set can be had in a neighbourhood hairdresser's at about half the price of a salon offering *haute coiffure*. Service is included at all hairdressing establishments. Men will find hairdressers and barbers in any neighbourhood. See page 103 for rates.

haircut	**coupe**
shampoo and set	**shampooing et mise en plis**
permanent wave	**permanente**
blow dry (brushing)	**brushing**
colour rinse/dye	**un rinçage/une teinture**
colour chart	**un nuancier, méchier**
Not too much off (here).	**Pas trop court (ici).**
A little more off (here).	**Un peu plus court (ici).**

HIKING *(tourisme pédestre)*. Whether you're already an experienced globe-trotter or you'd just like to have a closer look at the lakeside, vine-yards or mountains, there are extremely well-planned itineraries worked out by groups like the Association Valaisanne de Tourisme Pédestre and others seeking to promote a better knowledge of the more out-of-the-way villages and countryside. Little yellow signposts indicate directions and often give the estimated time of the walk. Detailed maps for hikers are available in bookstores, and the Office du Tourisme du

114

Canton de Vaud, Avenue de la Gare 10, 1002 Lausanne, has several
detailed brochures and maps which include routes in several cantons.
Tourist offices everywhere can give you information. See also POSTAL
BUSES.

HITCH-HIKING *(auto-stop).* Hitch-hiking is legal everywhere except
on the *autoroute* (motorway/expressway). On the whole, Switzerland is
a fairly good place to thumb your way around.

Can you give me a lift to…?	**Pouvez-vous m'emmener à…?**

HOTELS *(hôtel).* See also CAMPING and YOUTH HOSTELS. Hotels of all
categories are listed in the Swiss Hotel Guide (Guide suisse des hôtels)
issued by the Swiss Hotel Association and found at Swiss National
Tourist Offices in your country and in many travel agencies. Local
tourist offices also offer suggestions for accommodation in city hotels or
country inns *(auberge).*

Rates include taxes and service as well as a continental breakfast.
You must show your passport and fill out forms when registering.
Remember that prices are usually per person, and not only for the room
itself. For some average rates see page 103.

a single/double room with bath/shower	**une chambre à un lit/à deux lits avec bains/douche**
What's the rate per night?	**Quel est le tarif pour une nuit?**

HOURS *(heures d'ouverture).* Most offices and shops are open from
8 or 9 a.m. until 12 noon, then from 1.30 or 2 p.m. until 5 p.m. for
offices and until 6.30 or 7 p.m. for shops, Mondays to Fridays. Every
town has a half-day closing (Monday mornings or Thursday afternoons in Geneva and Lausanne). Small shops normally close for lunch.
On Saturday most shops are open non-stop from around 8 a.m. until
5 or 5.30 p.m. See also BANKS.

LANGUAGE. Four languages are officially used in Switzerland—Ger-
man *(Schwyzerdütsch),* French, Italian and Romansh, a rare Rhaeto-
Romanic offshoot of Latin. In this situation it's only natural that the
Swiss tend to be apt at learning foreign languages, and many speak
English well enough to help you find your way around or give limited
information, especially if you speak slowly. You're more likely to find
English-speaking people in Geneva, a very international city, than in
other parts of French-speaking Switzerland.

L

The Berlitz phrase book FRENCH FOR TRAVELLERS covers almost all situations you're likely to encounter in your travels in French-speaking Switzerland. In addition, the Berlitz French–English/English–French pocket dictionary contains a glossary of 12,500 terms plus a menu reader supplement.

Good morning/Good afternoon	**Bonjour**
Good afternoon/Good evening	**Bonsoir**
Thank you	**Merci**
Please	**S'il vous plaît**
Goodbye	**Au revoir**
Do you speak English?	**Parlez-vous anglais?**
I don't speak French.	**Je ne parle pas français.**

LAUNDRY and DRY CLEANING. If you want to have a load of clothes washed, look under *salons-lavoirs* in the telephone directory. For shirts or other items which need more attention, go to a *blanchisserie*.

For dry cleaning you have the choice between longer, more careful (and more expensive) or fast service which may take as little as a couple of hours. You should look for establishments called *nettoyage à sec* or, in the telephone book, *nettoyage chimique*.

When will it be ready?	**Quand est-ce que ce sera prêt?**
I must have it this afternoon/ tomorrow morning.	**Il me le faut pour cet après-midi/ demain matin.**

LOST PROPERTY. Check first with your hotel receptionist if you lose anything, then report the loss to the nearest police station. For property lost on trains or buses you should go to their *bureau des objets trouvés* (lost property office). A reward equivalent to 10 per cent is paid to the finder, especially when it concerns money, but a small fee is asked for most other objects.

I've lost my wallet/handbag/ passport.	**J'ai perdu mon porte-monnaie/ mon sac à main/mon passeport.**

M

MAIL *(poste).* If you don't know your address in advance, you should have your mail sent to *poste restante* (general delivery) at the main post office, the *Poste centrale,* of the town where you'll be staying. You'll have to show your passport as identification when collecting mail. Following are some postal codes for the main post offices: Bienne 2500;

Geneva 1200; Lausanne 1000; Neuchâtel 2000 and Sion (Valais) 1950.
See also POST OFFICE.

| Have you received any mail for…? | **Avez-vous du courrier pour…?** |

MAPS. Road maps *(carte routière)* are on sale in stationers' and book shops; street plans *(plan de ville)* are given away in large banks or at the tourist offices. Regional maps, especially good for hikers, are also on sale (scale of 1:50,000 and 1:25,000).

The maps in this guide are by Hallwag, who also publish a map of Switzerland.

| a street plan | **un plan de ville** |
| a (road) map of this region | **une carte (routière) de cette région** |

MEDICAL CARE. See also EMERGENCIES. Most major resorts have clinics and all cities are served by modern, well-equipped hospitals. Since health care may be very expensive, your insurance company at home can advise you about a policy covering illness or accident on holiday; or your travel agent will put you in touch with one of the Swiss insurance firms.

For minor ailments, any Swiss pharmacist *(pharmacien)* can recommend and supply certain medicines, and advise you where to find a doctor.

I need a doctor/dentist.	**Il me faut un médecin/un dentiste.**
I have a pain here.	**J'ai mal ici.**
I have a sore throat/a fever.	**J'ai mal à la gorge/de la fièvre.**

MEETING PEOPLE. The Swiss, though friendly, tend to be reserved. It may take some persistence to make contact. The scene is more relaxed in the resorts, and in general the cities offer activities where you can meet people.

When you enter and leave small shops or offices be sure to say *bonjour* (good morning, hello) or *bonsoir* (good afternoon, evening). Don't forget the appropriate please *(s'il vous plaît)* and thank you *(merci)*. See also LANGUAGE.

NEWSPAPERS and MAGAZINES *(journal; magazine)*. Even in small towns news-stands stock a surprising variety of foreign papers, plus all the Swiss newspapers in three major national languages. The best selection and earliest delivery are offered by main railway stations and airports. In large towns major British newspapers and the American *International Herald Tribune* (printed in Zurich) are widely available, along with American and British magazines of all kinds.

| Have you any English-language newspapers/magazines? | **Avez-vous des journaux/magazines en anglais?** |

P **PHOTOGRAPHY.** Swiss dealers handle all popular film brands and sizes. Photo shops in the larger ski resorts develop and print black-and-white film, but colour film usually has to be mailed to city labs. Major stores also accept film for processing.

I'd like a film for this camera.	**J'aimerais un film pour cet appareil.**
How long will it take to develop this film?	**Combien de temps faut-il pour développer ce film?**
a black-and-white film	**un film noir et blanc**
a film for colour prints	**un film couleurs**
a colour-slide film	**un film pour diapositives**

POLICE *(police).* Law and order is the responsibility of the cantonal police *(police cantonale* or *gendarmerie)* and of the local city police *(police municipale).* For accidents, loss, theft or other emergencies call 117 to be connected with the nearest police station.

| Where's the nearest police station? | **Où est le poste de police le plus proche?** |

POSTAL BUSES *(car postal).* Wherever the trains don't go, the postal buses do. They carry the mail as well as the local population and tourists who'd rather not have to drive such difficult roads or who like to visit out-of-the-way places. There are weekly or monthly tickets which offer great reductions on any of the postal bus routes.

The *service postal des voyageurs* has also drawn up 30 hiking itineraries in Valais combined with postal bus services. Brochures and schedules can be obtained at any post office or the tourist office. See also Swiss Holiday Card.

POST OFFICE and TELEGRAMS *(poste; télégramme).* See also Mail and Telephone. Post offices are recognized by their distinctive sign showing a white cross on a red background and the letters PTT (Poste, Téléphone, Télégraphe) in black. They handle telephone calls and telegrams as well as postal services. Normal business hours are from 7.30 a.m. to noon and 1.30 to 6.30 p.m., Mondays to Fridays and on Saturday mornings from 7.30 to 11 a.m. In major towns the main post office does not close for lunch.

Stamps *(timbre)* are also sold from vending machines outside post offices or at the train station in some towns. Or you can buy them in souvenir shops and at hotel desks. Letter boxes are yellow. Large towns have an "emergency" mail service. A window of one main post office stays open late and on weekends to accept special delivery or express mail or parcels. In Lausanne this window is at Avenue de la Gare, 43bis, open until 10 p.m. In Geneva the post office is next to the train station on the Rue de Lausanne, open until 10.45 p.m.

Main post offices accept telegrams from 7 a.m. to 10 p.m. To phone in a telegram call from your hotel, where the cost is added to your bill, dial 110.

express (special delivery)	**exprès**
airmail	**par avion**
registered	**recommandé**
A stamp for this letter/postcard, please.	**Un timbre pour cette lettre/carte postale, s'il vous plaît.**
I want to send a telegram to...	**J'aimerais envoyer un télégramme à...**

PRICES. For an idea of what things cost, see the section PLANNING YOUR BUDGET on page 103. You may return home raving about many aspects of your Swiss holiday, but not the bargains. With few exceptions the prices are higher than at home, sometimes very much so although quality is high too. But to keep the country competitive as a holiday destination, the travel trade has frozen its own prices, especially in the hotel sector. Some prices may be higher in Geneva, but generally they vary only slightly from one region to another. Of course you'd expect to pay more in a fashionable boutique in a chic resort than in a large store in any town.

PUBLIC HOLIDAYS. The calendar of holidays varies from canton to canton, so ask for a complete list when you stop by the local tourist office. Banks and shops are liable to be closed a full or half day on August 1 (National Day) and for certain religious or cantonal celebrations. The following holidays are observed in all French-speaking cantons except those indicated (see also inside back cover):

P

January 1	*Nouvel An*	New Year's Day
December 25	*Noël*	Christmas Day
Movable dates:	*Vendredi-Saint*	Good Friday (except Valais)
	Lundi de Pâques	Easter Monday
	Ascension	Ascension
	Lundi de Pentecôte	Whit Monday (except Valais)

Are you open tomorrow? **Ouvrez-vous demain?**

R **RADIO and TV** *(radio; télévision).* Radio Suisse Internationale (short-wave) broadcasts news in English from Berne at 7 p.m. every day of the week plus commentaries at 7.15 p.m. from Monday to Friday. You can tune in on the radio in your hotel room (télédiffusion programme 1). Also on shortwave, you can get the BBC, Voice of America and Radio Canada International. The American Armed Forces Network broadcasts on medium wave frequencies.

There are sports events, concerts and operas presented on Swiss TV either in French, German or Italian.

RELIGIOUS SERVICES. Switzerland is almost equally divided between Roman Catholics and Protestants. Major cities have religious services for many other denominations; English and American congregations are found in bigger towns and resorts.

The following addresses might be useful:

Geneva: English Church of the Holy Trinity, Rue du Mont-Blanc, tel. (022) 315155.

American Emmanual Episcopal, Rue de Monthoux 3, tel. (022) 328078.

Calvin Auditorium (Presbyterian), next to Cathedral, 1, Place de la Taconnerie. English service: 9.30 a.m. Sundays.

English-speaking Roman Catholic Mission, Avenue William Favre 36, tel. (022) 368208.

Lausanne: Scots Kirk, British and American Presbyterian congregation, Avenue de Rumine 26, tel. (021) 239828.

Church of England, Avenue de l'Eglise-Anglaise 1, tel. (021) 262636.

English-speaking Catholic Community, Avenue de Béthusy 54A,
120 tel. (021) 334258.

SKI-EQUIPMENT HIRE *(location d'un équipement de ski).* All sports shops rent cross-country and downhill ski, skating and other equipment, and if you're coming to Switzerland by plane you'll find it more convenient to hire your gear at your final destination. For prices see page 103.

SWISS HOLIDAY CARD. You can criss-cross the whole country by train, bus and boat with a Swiss Holiday Card *(carte suisse de vacances).* This covers the whole Swiss federal railway network, plus some 79 private railways, 9 boat companies, 120 postal bus routes, along with discounts on other means of transport, like many mountain railways and aerial cableways, granting a reduction of around 25 per cent. First-class tickets cost approximately 40 per cent more than second class ones (see p. 103). Children from 6 to 16 pay half price. You can buy the card from just about any Swiss national tourist office abroad (see TOURIST INFORMATION OFFICES), as well as in Switzerland itself from railways stations in major towns. Note that you'll have to show proof that you're non-resident in Switzerland to get the ticket. You must therefore produce your passport when applying for a Holiday Card.

TAXI *(taxi).* Rates vary from town to town but are never very low. You won't be overcharged; cabs are metered and there are set prices (displayed in the cab) for extras such as baggage. Hailing taxis on the street is possible, but there are taxi ranks in front of main train stations and the centre of town. You can call one at 141 in Geneva and Lausanne or by looking under *Taxi* in the phone directory. In some towns, tips are not included (but the fact will be indicated in some evident spot inside); if this is the case, 10 to 15 per cent is normal.

TELEGRAMS—see **POST OFFICE**

TELEPHONE *(téléphone).* Through the efficient Swiss telephone network you can dial most of the world directly, even from a public telephone box. Instructions in four languages, including English, are posted in all of them.

Most telephone booths have directories for each canton, but if not ring 111 for information. There are usually instructions in English in the blue front-pages of each directory. Telephones are also found in all post offices where you can either use an automatic phone or make your call and pay at the window afterwards.

121

T **TIME DIFFERENCES.** Switzerland is on Central European Time (GMT+1) like most of the Continent. The winter chart looks thus:

New York	London	Switzerland	Jo'burg	Sydney	Auckland
6 a.m.	11 a.m.	**noon**	1 p.m.	10 p.m.	midnight

Summer time comes into force on the same days as for Switzerland's neighbours.

TIPPING. Tipping has been abolished in Swiss restaurants and hotels so an added tip to the waiter or chamber maid is optional—although for good service it will always be appreciated. Porters on the other hand, should be given 1 or 2 francs per bag.

TOILETS. Throughout Switzerland you'll find exceptionally clean public toilets at convenient locations, as well as in large stores and all cafés and restaurants. The conventional symbols for men's and women's rooms, or the expressions *toilettes* or *WC* are often used. Otherwise look for the signs *dames* for women and *messieurs* for men.

Where are the toilets?   **Où sont les toilettes?**

TOURIST INFORMATION OFFICES *(office du tourisme).* All Swiss resorts and larger towns have their own local tourist office ready to supply free brochures, hotel lists and other information. Some of the following addresses might be useful:

Fribourg: Tourist Office, Grands-Places 30, tel. (037) 813175/76.

Geneva: Tourist Office, Rue des Moulins 2, tel. (022) 287233.
Swiss Student Travel Office, Rue Vignier 3, tel. (022) 299733.

Lausanne: Tourist Office (A.D.I.L.), Avenue d'Ouchy 60, tel. (021) 277321.
Office de Tourisme du Canton de Vaud, Avenue de la Gare 10, tel. (021) 227782.
Swiss Student Travel Office, Rue de la Barre 8, tel. (021) 203975.

Neuchâtel: Tourist Office (A.D.E.N.), Place Numa-Droz 1, tel. (038) 254242.

Sion: Union Valaisanne du Tourisme, Rue de Lausanne 15, tel. (027) 223161.

In most major cities of Europe and North America, the Swiss National **T**
Tourist Office provides complete information to help you plan your
holiday.

Canada: Commerce Court West, Suite 2015 (P.O. Box 215),
Toronto, Ont. M5L 1E8; tel.: (416) 868-0584.

South Africa: Agency with Swissair (performs the function of a
tourist office). Swiss House, 86 Main Street, P.O.B.
3866, Johannesburg; tel.: (011) 836 9941.

United Kingdom: Swiss Centre, 1, New Coventry Street, London W1V
3HG; tel.: (01) 734-1921

U.S.A.: The Swiss Center, 608 Fifth Avenue, New York, NY
10020; tel.: (212) 757-5944.
250 Stockton Street, San Francisco, CA 94108; tel.:
(415) 362-2260.

In Switzerland you'll find the head branch of the National Tourist
Office at Bellariastrasse 38, 8027 Zurich, tel. (01) 20 23737.

Where's the tourist office?   **Où est l'office du tourisme?**

TRAINS *(train)*. Swiss trains are fast, clean, comfortable and very
punctual. If there are any delays, they usually come after heavy snow-
falls. Trains leave at regular hourly intervals between all major centres
within the country.

TEE	The international Trans-Europ-Express, first class, only with surcharge; seat reservations mandatory.
Train interville	«Intercity» air-conditioned express train for direct connections between the major cities (no surcharge).
Train direct	Express train stopping at medium-sized towns.
Train accéléré	Train providing express shuttle service between medium-sized towns.
Train régional	Local train stopping at all stations.

123

T

Wagon-lits Sleeping-car with 1-, 2- or 3-bed compartments and wash basins (on international trains passing through Switzerland)	Couchette Sleeping-berth car with blankets, sheets and pillows	Wagon-restaurant Dining-car on express trains

In addition to the federal railways (SBB/CFF/FFS), a number of small independent lines serve certain of the country's most isolated areas. Some of these, such as the Blonay-Chamby or the MOB (Montreux–Oberland Bernois) are tourist attractions in their own right. See also POSTAL BUSES.

If you jump onto a train just as it leaves, without a ticket, the inspector will sell you one at a slight surcharge. Remember children from 6 to 16 pay half price. For sample fares see page 103.

When's the next train to...?	**A quelle heure part le prochain train pour...?**
I'd like to make a seat reservation.	**J'aimerais réserver une place.**
first/second class	**première/deuxième classe**
single (one-way)/return (round-trip)	**aller simple/aller-retour**

W WATER *(eau)*. Ice-cold Alpine village water, fresh from the tap, is a delicious thirst-quencher bearing little resemblance to town water. The tap water in Swiss cities is perfectly adequate, but with meals the custom is to order a bottle of mineral water—and wine.

a bottle of mineral water	**une bouteille d'eau minérale**
carbonated/non-carbonated	**gazeuse/non gazeuse**

Y YOUTH HOSTELS *(auberge de jeunesse)*. Young people up to the age of 25 can stay in these low-priced dormitories, and parents of any age can also accompany their children if they are members of a youth hostel association. Advance booking is recommended in summer, or in regions where winter sports abound. Certain hostels in cities are closed during the winter months. For a complete list of addresses and regulations, contact the Schweizerischer Bund für Jugendherbergen, Hochhaus 9, Shopping-Center, Postfach 132, 8958 Spreitenbach. Local youth hostels

124

are listed in the phone book under *auberge de jeunesse*. Student accommodation is often available in university towns and some resorts; for information, apply to the Swiss Student Travel Office, Rue Vignier 3, Geneva, tel. (022) 299733 or in Lausanne at Rue de la Barre 8 (behind the cathedral), tel. (021) 203975. You can get information from the head office in Zurich by calling (01) 2423131. This organization publishes a guide called *Switzerland the Cheap Way*.

SOME USEFUL EXPRESSIONS

yes/no	**oui/non**
please/thank you	**s'il vous plaît/merci**
excuse me	**excusez-moi**
you're welcome	**je vous en prie**
where/when/how	**où/quand/comment**
how long/how far	**combien de temps/à quelle distance**
yesterday/today/tomorrow	**hier/aujourd'hui/demain**
day/week/month/year	**jour/semaine/mois/année**
left/right	**gauche/droite**
up/down	**en haut/en bas**
good/bad	**bon/mauvais**
big/small	**grand/petit**
cheap/expensive	**bon marché/cher**
hot/cold	**chaud/froid**
old/new	**vieux/neuf**
open/closed	**ouvert/fermé**
Does anyone here speak English?	**Y a-t-il quelqu'un ici qui parle anglais?**
I don't understand.	**Je ne comprends pas.**
Please write it down.	**Veuillez bien me l'écrire.**
What does this mean?	**Que signifie ceci?**
Help me, please.	**Aidez-moi, s'il vous plaît.**
What time is it?	**Quelle heure est-il?**
I'd like…	**J'aimerais...**
How much is that?	**C'est combien?**
Waiter!/Waitress!	**S'il vous plaît!**

Index

An asterisk (*) next to a page number indicates a map reference.